Paul Barber was born in Liverpool in 1951. Best known for his roles as Denzil in *Only Fools and Horses* and Horse in *The Full Monty*, he has appeared in numerous TV favourites such as *Coronation Street*, *Holby City*, *Brookside* and *Taggart*. Other film credits include *The Long Good Friday*, *The 51st State* and, most recently, *Dead Man's Cards*.

FOSTER KID

Paul Barber, the actor best known for his roles as Denzil in *Only Fools and Horses* and Horse in *The Full Monty*, grew up in 1950s Liverpool. After the death of his mother, Paul and his brothers and sister spent the rest of their childhood in a succession of children's and foster homes. Paul left care at the age of sixteen, and three years later landed his first acting role, by accident, in the musical *Hair* which put him on the path to London and a successful career in show business. *Foster Kid* is a frank, sometimes funny, account of a young boy's life spent in care, his troubled youth and how one lucky break got him to where he is today.

PAUL BARBER

FOSTER KID
A Liverpudlian Childhood

Complete and Unabridged

CHARNWOOD
Leicester

First published in Great Britain in 2007 by
Sphere
an imprint of
Little, Brown Book Group
London

First Charnwood Edition
published 2008
by arrangement with
Little, Brown Book Group
London

British Library CIP Data

Barber, Paul, *1952* –
    Foster kid: a Liverpudlian childhood.—
    Large print ed.—Charnwood library series
    1. Barber, Paul, *1952* – 2. Television actors and
    actresses—Great Britain—Biography 3. Foster
    children—England—Liverpool—Biography
    4. Large type books
    I. Title
    791.4'5'028'092

    ISBN 978–1–84782–304–5

Published by
F. A. Thorpe (Publishing)
Anstey, Leicestershire
Set by Words & Graphics Ltd.
Anstey, Leicestershire
Printed and bound in Great Britain by
T. J. International Ltd., Padstow, Cornwall

This book is printed on acid-free paper

For my mother, Margaret Bartley

Acknowledgements

I started writing down memories about my early life back in 1986 and when I had finished I showed the manuscript to Miles Warde, and subsequently talked about it on the radio programme *Off the Page* with Matthew Parris. So, first of all, I would first like to say thank you to them, for without that exposure this book may never have seen the light of day.

A massive thank you to Elise Dillsworth, my editor, confidante and, most of all, friend who has tirelessly helped, guided and supported me on this long and sometimes arduous journey. We finally got there. (Oh, and thank you for the morsels of bread and water!)

Thank you to my family: Claudette and family, Lorraine and family, Brian and Annette, Mike, Paul, Simon (nifty fingers) and Reanne, Ben and Pauline. Thank you all for being there for me and loving me. It really means a lot.

A big and warm thank you to all my friends who have stuck by me and spurred me on: Angela Bruce and Sonali Fernando, Helen (fruit) Demetriou and family, Alan and Beryl Williams, Larrington Walker, Tony Lovendeer, Jamshid and family, Cyril and family, Jane and family, the Giles family, Mena and Al Heywood. Nick and Sue, and my bestest friend Paul Giles.

And a very special thank you to my former

agent Bill Horne who gave me my first typewriter, and last but by no means least, Jean Diamond, my manager and special friend.

God Bless you all.

Prologue

They gave me the bumps like you would give your friends on their birthday in the school playground — only it wasn't my birthday. It was my leaving day. I was finally leaving the care system, which I had been in since the age of seven. Ten bumps — nine for each year and an extra one for luck.

Sydney House was a working hostel for young boys who had come up through the care system, outgrown the children's homes or moved on from their foster parents. In reality it was a halfway house, the last stop before stepping out into a brave new world. I was saying goodbye to my friends, boys like Alan, Pat, Robbie, Stephen, John and Ray, and staff members who were put in charge of us and prepared us for the adult world we were about to enter — Mr Aspinall, Mr Mitchell and Mr Culshaw, Mr A, Mr M and Mr C, respectively, as we liked to call them. Mr A ran the hostel like a captain running a tight ship. There was nothing fancy about the home or even the rooms, just the bare essentials. It was a fairly large house situated in a greenly suburb of Liverpool. The few clothes I had bought myself with my wages, the records I had started to collect and my very first record player were the only possessions I was taking with me. The decision to leave was not my own, but that of the local authorities who deemed that when you reached the age of eighteen you were a young adult and it was time for them to let you go. Strange as it may seem, although I was glad to be leaving, I was going to miss being in care. The thought of all those years in care, the many friends and staff I had come to know and love, left me feeling somewhat saddened now that I was leaving them all behind. Mr C and Mr M had joined in with the rest of my friends in giving me the bumps as I playfully struggled to break free from them. I felt like a hero who had just scored the winning goal, trying my best to be modest about it all, trying to play it down, trying to be cool, but they weren't having any of it. They gripped my arms and legs tightly, raising my body into the air before letting it fall on to the grassy lawn with a thud, only to do it again and again and again.

'Come on, Paddy, take it like a man,' Robbie shouted. Then they all started to sing: 'For he's a jolly good fellow.' It was the first time in ages that I was overcome with emotion. Mr A stood watching from the doorway, a big proud grin on his face. It was quite common for the boys to end up joining one of the forces — Royal Navy, air force, army or the merchant navy — and in my case it might well have been the merchant navy if it had not been for Mr C's words of advice and encouragement, telling me to take my chances on land instead. Had I not listened to him my life might have turned out quite differently. But this is how it did happen. As my bum crashed to the ground for the tenth time, memories came flooding back as if it was all only yesterday.

1

I was born on 18 March 1951 to Margaret and Samuel Kay Barber in Crown Street, Liverpool, the youngest of five children. First came Paul, followed by Claudette, Brian and Michael. I was christened Patrick and took on the name of Paul (my confirmation name, taken from my eldest brother, and not from St Paul) many years later when I became an actor. My father died on 17 March 1953, just one day before my second birthday. The little I know about him came from the information on his death certificate; he was a retired merchant seaman from Freetown, Sierra Leone, and had died of pulmonary tuberculosis. After his death we moved to a third-floor, one-room flat in Upper Canning Street. The landing had a communal gas stove, bathroom and toilet, but we didn't have to share these as the old lady who lived on the same floor had died. Once we sneaked into her room to have a look around and Claudy took some false nails she had found. Our room was dominated by a large, dark, ornate dresser with a mirror in the centre, and it housed the cutlery and foodstuffs such as bread, biscuits, salt and pepper, tea and coffee. Alongside the dresser was a large double bed. Mum and Claudy slept at the top end and Paul, Brian and Michael at the bottom. I had my cot. We had one wardrobe which was next to the fireplace and a dining table with four high-backed chairs and two armchairs in front of the fireplace. This was my home. My earliest memories are stored like a silent movie: I just sat quietly and watched my family coming and going in and out of the room, until their voices became familiar and recognisable, as did those coming out of the radio, which was on just about all day and every day.

Claudette, Paul, Brian and Michael were forever running in and out, asking what was for tea, if they could go out and play on the swings in Myrtle Street or go round to an aunt or uncle; sometimes they stopped over and stayed the night. These aunts and uncles were really just friends of Mum's. Her female friends were mostly white and her male friends were mostly black, of West African origin, so we knew they weren't related, but we would always call them auntie and uncle, out of respect and because of our closeness to them. When my brothers and sister were at school, Mum would sometimes take me out — to the park, shopping or to visit one of her friends. I remember once when we went to visit Auntie Maize. I wanted to go outside as it was hot so Mum said I could play on the front steps where they could both keep an eye on me. After a while I was called inside for my tea. Auntie Maize picked me up and said, 'Are you hungry, Paddy? Would you like some lettuce to eat?' I smiled and said, 'Yes, please.' I waited at the table, playing with my wooden fish, broom-brooming as I weaved it in and out of the spaces between the various things on the table.

4

Then Auntie Maize put a plate in front of me with a lot of green, wrinkly leaves, cold sliced eggs and some bread and Mum handed me a cup of lemonade. I started to gulp it down, staring at the plate and not quite sure what to do with it as it didn't look very nice. I started to cry.

'What's the matter, Paddy?' asked Mum.

I shoved the plate away, trying to explain between tears and hiccups that I thought Auntie Maize was going to give me some letters to read. Though I didn't understand why this made them burst into fits of laughter, I was glad I was making them smile.

Most evenings were spent sitting round the fire listening to the radio, which was always tuned to Radio Luxembourg ('Your Station of the Stars'). Claudette was about six, only a couple of years older than Michael, but she would always help Mum with the household chores and with getting Michael and me ready for bed. She would get the tin bath from the corner of the room and place it in front of the fireplace, then fill the kettle and place it directly on to the fire and wait for it to boil, then pour the water into the bath, holding the hot handle with old newspaper. On the nights that we didn't have a bath she would just strip-wash us, which meant we had to stand on a chair in front of the fire so that she didn't have to stoop down all the time, and she would wash our arms and legs with a flannel and we'd stay there till we'd dried off. I hated having my hair combed and must have driven our Claudy round the bend. First of all she had to catch me, and, being so small, I was able to dodge her by hiding under the table where she couldn't get at me. Eventually, losing patience with me, she would go over to the bed where Mum was sleeping, threatening me with 'If I have to wake Mum up you will be for it'. I would remain under the table, defiant, refusing to budge. 'Right, that's it,' she would say. Rousing Mum from her slumber she would say, 'Mum, Paddy won't let me comb his hair; he's under the table again' at which point I would emerge after Mum had warned me she wouldn't take me to the park or the swings, or something else, if I didn't behave.

Sometimes, to amuse ourselves, we would play-act and one time Claudy and Brian decided they were going to be a queen and king for a day and re-enact the Coronation. Brian grabbed the table-cloth and emptied the sugar bowl into a piece of newspaper, then turned it upside down so that the upturned legs looked like little crucifixes and it resembled a crown. Claudy was seated in all her splendour, wrapped in the white table-cloth-cum-cloak, covered with telltale food marks: blotches of tomato ketchup, breadcrumbs, sugar-encrusted Echo margarine stains. Brian walked towards her with great seriousness and passion, holding the sugar bowl aloft, and then brought it crashing down on her head. Claudy burst out crying, but managed to compose herself and then, with queen-like dignity, proceeded to beat seven kinds of shit out of the king.

There was a year's difference in age between all of us except Paul who was eight, two years older than Claudy. Paul was hardly ever at home, but when he was he and Mum always seemed to be at odds with each other. One day I was standing in my cot and I became aware that the voices in the room were becoming louder and louder. Michael was looking out of the window and Paul was standing in the middle of the room shouting at Mum. The next thing I saw was Mum picking up a knife and throwing it straight at Paul. He immediately ducked, giving the knife a clear path towards Michael who had now turned round but was unable to move out of the way quick enough. The knife hit him just above his left eye before falling to the floor. Mum rushed over to Michael and shouted at Paul again. A few days later Paul was no longer with us. As I got a bit older I would often ask Mum where Paul was; she would tell me he was staying at an aunt's and that we couldn't see him just yet, but soon.

I was fascinated by the other voices in the room besides our own, some of which sang as well. I would hear songs like 'Oh Rose Marie', Mantovani's 'Cascading strings', 'Que Sera Sera', and listen to Horace Batchelor going on about his 'Infra-draw' football pools system every night. I loved these voices and wanted to know where they lived. And then one day it just hit me: the voices, the music, the sounds of horses galloping away were all coming from the wireless on the dresser. I wanted to meet all these beautiful people and decided to make my way round to the back of the wireless. No one else was in, but Mum had told Uncle Sam to pop round and check on me. I climbed on to a chair

7

and pulled the radio towards me and looked at the back of it. I was very disappointed to see nothing but some old dusty wires and valves and no tiny people inside walking about and singing, so I quickly turned my attention to something that had caught my eye at the very top of the dresser: it was a large jar of dark, syrupy, thick liquid that Mum gave me spoons of from time to time. I climbed from the chair right on to the dresser and reached up to grasp the bottom of the jar. Then the dresser started to lean forward and I realised that I wasn't going to make it back to the chair below. Just then there was a knock on the door and, as the unit started to fall towards the floor, I screamed in panic. The door burst open and there stood Uncle Sam, a tall, dark figure in a light brown gaberdine overcoat, a large brown hat, dark glasses and with a white cane. The first thing he did was to put his arm out in front of him to stop the dresser — and me — crashing to the ground, and then lifted me off the unit and gently put me back on the floor. He put everything back in its place on the dresser, including the radio and then tapped his way towards the armchair by the fire, sat down and nodded off. I'd been saved by a blind man. When Mum returned Uncle Sam said nothing except, 'I could do with a nice cup of tea.'

Even though I don't have any photographs of her I remember Mum as being beautiful. I would say she was a cross between Rita Hayworth and Claudette Colbert. I always remember her in her fifties costume: pencil skirt and short coat. I used to love watching her putting on her make-up and getting ready to go out. She would put the panstick on, pencil in her eyebrows and then apply ruby-red lipstick. I would be standing in my cot, fascinated. Just before she left she would kiss us goodnight, turning out the light and leaving us in the cosy room, semi-lit by the glow of the fire. The radio was left on low, which would most times send us to sleep. Other times, not long after Mum had left, Brian and Claudy would get up, get dressed and follow her, leaving Michael and me on our own.

As I got older I would join them and hang around outside the pub, whatever the weather. Someone would tell Mum that her kids were outside and she would come out and tell us to get back home. We would have these excuses: 'Mum, the rent man's at the door so we thought we would come and tell you', 'Mum, the fire's gone out', 'Mum, I can't sleep.' She would laugh as if to say nice try, then she would go back inside and a few moments later she would send out bottles of pop and packets of peanuts, with instructions to wait for her. And when she did finally come out from the pub she would take us all home, stopping off at the chippy on the way and getting fourpennyworth of chips and a loaf of crusts, which were the end bits of loaves of bread. She would have her hair in rollers tied up in a scarf and wearing her gaberdine mac, and she still looked good. She spent whatever money she had on us kids but there must have been times when she wanted something just for herself — be it food or time. I remember one occasion when it was the former. One day she decided to treat herself to something special to eat. None of us were hungry as we had already eaten. When Mum brought her plate into the room Claudette whispered to me to ask Mum if it was for us. When I did, Mum threw the contents of the plate on to the fire and yelled at me, 'For Christ's sake, Paddy Barber, can't I have a bit of food to myself?' I felt rotten and Claudette had beaten a hasty retreat to the other side of the room.

Things had probably got on top of her that day; earlier on, Mum had taken us all to see Mrs Wiseman, a Jewish lady who had a clothes shop in one of the houses a few streets away from us. She was well known and very popular with a lot of poor families in the area, as the big shops in the town centre were far too expensive for most people, and our family was no exception. She had kitted us out with new duffel coats, shirts and trousers, sandals and shoes. On our way home, Mum popped into the local shop for some groceries. She had bought some eggs, which she had left momentarily on top of our new duffel coats on a chair. Michael, wearing his new trousers, sat down on the chair with the brand new coats on it, and also the bag of eggs. Michael was up to his behind in broken eggs and Mum was not pleased.

When I was four years old I joined Brian and Claudy at Windsor Street School. I remember Mum taking me to school for the first time, making my sandwiches and giving me money wrapped up in a piece of paper for my milk and biscuits, just as she had done with Brian before me. The school was very mixed, with children of all races, and I was never aware of being different as there were loads of kids with the same complexion as me. It was a real melting pot. The school was quite large and had three playgrounds: a very small one for the infants at the front of the school, one for the juniors to the rear and one on the roof, which was just for the girls. Claudy wasn't living with us by this time and had gone to stay with an aunt. At playtime she would look down through the railings from the roof and call to us, just to check that we were OK.

At dinnertime we were given little blue tickets and taken across the road to the dinner centres. We would queue up outside and wait for the other kids from the school at the other end of Windsor Street to finish and then we would go in and have ours.

Most mornings on our way to school we would get up to all kinds of mischief. We would go up to people's doorsteps, break open the tops of milk bottles, take a few swigs and then leave the bottle on its side and let the rest of the milk flow down the steps and into the gullies and then run away. We would also stop off at the local sweetshop run by Mrs Rimmer, a little lady who wore glasses and who had a distinctive white streak in her hair. We would always buy our sweets and she always gave us extra ones, so it never entered our heads to steal from her. Sometimes on our way home from school we would cut through a little park in Huskisson Street and sit with the park keeper who would share his sandwiches with us and give us hot cups of tea from his jerry can. He was known as the cocky watchman: he was always keeping an eye out in case anyone got up to mischief.

I soon lost interest in school lessons — not that I learnt much anyway — so I started to sag, to bunk off school. I only began to do this when I realised as I was making my way home alone that there was no one to meet me after school. I was familiar with my surroundings now and able to find my own way around the area. There was always somewhere for me to go, somewhere to play and explore. I found favourite places, old ruined houses that had been bombed during the war, waste ground down by the cathedral littered with abandoned cars and clapped-out dinner vans with 'Liverpool Education Committee' painted on the sides. Hours and hours I would spend playing on them, pretending to drive them, and when I tired of playing there I would move on to somewhere else.

Sometimes when I was playing down by Pier Head I would jump on the ferry and spend hours going back and forth across the Mersey without actually getting off or paying for the journey. I would just hide under the seats. One time I fell asleep and when I woke up it was dark. I jumped off the boat and didn't recognise any of the streets. I looked around for a familiar landmark and spotted the Anglican cathedral. As I ran towards it I realised it was on the other side of the Mersey. I was lost. I began to panic and thought of Mum worrying about where I was. As I walked through the streets I started to cry, my

12

sobs getting louder with each step. Then a woman opened her front door and asked me what was wrong. She took me inside and gave me some crumpets with melted butter and called the police. Needless to say, Mum wasn't in the best of moods when I got home.

When I sagged school and spent time in town, I would drop by the barrow boys who worked selling fruit and veg and ask them if they had any Penny Fades, which were apples that were slightly damaged or faded. Sure enough one of them would bring out a small knife from a pocket, cut away the spoilt bit and give me the apples free of charge.

The first time I ever went to the circus was when I was sagging school. One afternoon my brothers and I sneaked out of the playground, almost bent double below the wall, and off up the road, and this giant man in a top hat came stalking up the street. When he got to us he reached down and handed us tickets for the show. We followed him all the way to the Princess Park where the circus and the fair were, and when we got there there was this big grey elephant just floating in the air. I was agog, speechless, and in awe of what I was seeing, all these happy people gathered in one place. There was lots of things to go on and we ate sweets — rock, candyfloss and, my favourite, toffee apples.

There was always a sense of excitement and adventure for me in those early days at home with Mum and my brothers and sister. Because Michael and me were the youngest we tended to stay together as we could never keep up with Brian and Claudy. They were always running off to the park or to the swings, or going to see their friends. Sometimes after dinner at school we would bunk off and take the rest of the afternoon off and go and do our own thing. We sometimes spent whole afternoons visiting Uncle Tefra, not a real uncle but another friend of Mum's. He lived just around the corner from the school and was a retired merchant seaman from West Africa. He always welcomed us into his house, always had time for us. He would put the kettle on, give us big mugs of tea with lots of condensed milk in it, and then make us crispy bacon sandwiches. We would sit there listening to the radio and sometimes he would give us a little job to do, like polishing his shoes, and he always paid us for it. There was a certain way he wanted his shoes shined. He would take the brush in his left hand and the shoe in the right, then he would brush the shoe and as he did so rock his head in time with each stroke of the brush. And when we did it he would laugh out loud.

There was a garage that we passed every day and Claudy used to open the small door which was set into the larger one and shout obscenities at the men inside. They would come and chase us as we ran away laughing. But one day Claudy wasn't fast enough and when the man slammed the door shut it caught the top of one of her fingers and took it right off. I'll never forget the look of horror on our Claudy's face. She became hysterical and screamed all the way to Uncle Tefra's house. It wasn't until he stuck her bloody hand under the cold-water tap that he realised that the top of her finger was missing.

'Oh my God!' he cried. 'Where is the top of your finger? How did this happen?' We stood there watching helplessly as he struggled to wrap Claudy's hand in a towel.

He told us to run home and tell Mum to meet him at Myrtle Street Hospital. Mum was on the landing, standing over the gas stove preparing our tea. We all started to speak at the same time. 'Mum, Mum, our Claudy's gone to the hospital with Uncle Tefra. He said you have to go and meet them there.' Brian was the most audible as me and Michael were too upset and distressed to speak clearly.

'Why, what's happened?' she said as she turned the stove off and came running into our room.

'Our Claudy's hurt her hand,' blurted out Brian.

'Right, you stay here and look after Michael and Paddy till I get back!' After Mum left, Brian turned to Michael and me and said, 'When Mum gets back from the hospital you two are to say nothing, OK?' We nodded our heads in agreement.

The next morning Mum took us all to school herself. When we got to the garage, Mum told us all to wait. She opened the small door, stepped inside, picked up the top of our Claudy's finger and stepped back out. Then she took out a Walker's toffee from her pocket, gave Michael the sweet and placed the tip of the finger into the empty wrapper. Nobody said a word as we continued on our way. Mum left us at the school gate and then took Claudy back to the hospital to see if the fingertip could be sewn back on, but it was dead after lying on the floor of the garage all night. That very same afternoon we were off sagging again, only this time we went home instead of heading into town. We wanted to see what the top of our Claudy's finger looked like not attached to the rest of her hand, but we never did see it again and we never really talked to Claudy about her missing fingertip.

Sometimes I sagged with our Michael as I wanted to see how he spent his afternoons and how he got money. It turned out that he would stop people in the street and ask them for cash. Then, once he had enough he would spend the rest of the afternoon watching cartoons at the Tatler Picture House. We would watch most of the cowboy pictures showing at the time starring Hopalong Cassidy, the Cisco Kid and Roy Rogers, and the funny men of the period, like Charlie Chaplin, Laurel and Hardy, the Three Stooges, the Dead End Kids and the Little Rascals. Sometimes we would queue along with the adults and ask them to take us in just so that we could watch a grown-up movie like *Island In The Sun*. Harry Belafonte and Joan Collins were in that one. We would go up to couples, ones with friendly-looking faces, and ask them to take us in. We'd tell them that our mum had given us the money for the tickets if they would buy them for us.

I quickly learnt how to get money not by begging but by acting. I would stand on the edge

16

of the pavement right by a drain, wait until a kind face came towards me and then, just as the person got within hearing range, I would turn on the waterworks and cry my eyes out. When he or she stopped to ask me what the matter was I would splutter that I had been running to get the bus home and my fare had fallen out of my hand and right down the drain. Convinced by my story, they would reach into their pockets or purses and give me either sixpences or threepenny bits. This scam didn't work every time, though. Once, someone who had fallen for the trick caught me going through the same act with another unsuspecting soul and told me to clear off. It was time to move to another part of town.

By now we were getting up to all kinds of mischief, not just outside but at home too. One day Michael and me were at home by ourselves, playing with our toys and listening to the radio, when we heard the rag and bone man passing by on his horsedrawn cart shouting, 'Any old iron, any old iron.' I immediately dived into the bottom drawer of the wardrobe where Mum kept a lot of old clothes and found a coat and some other items. I bundled them all together and ran down the stairs. Michael shouted after me that it wouldn't be a good idea and that I would be in for it when Mum got home. I ignored him and chased after the cart. Breathless, I handed everything over and asked the man for a climbing monkey on a stick, a windmill and a jar of Aunt Sally Bubbles! Fair enough, son, he said and he dipped into his sack and pulled out the goods and handed them over to me. Well, when Mum got home she went spare. I'd just traded her best fur coat.

Mum used to send us to do the messages — household shopping — and one time she sent me to one of the nearby corner shops. She had a list of groceries that she needed, like tea, sugar, Echo margarine, a bottle of sterry (sterilised milk) and loosies (single cigarettes). She wrapped the money inside the list and told me to keep tight hold of it and to hand it straight to the lady in the shop. The lady began to get items from off the shelves and put them into a brown carrier bag. I'd noticed that one of the items was a bottle of what looked like clear water stopped with a cork. I thought, 'Great, lemonade. I'll have a swig of that on my way home.' I took two big mouthfuls and immediately spat them out on to the street. As I was trying to get rid of the taste in my mouth I lost concentration of what I was doing and was dragging the shopping bag along the ground. By the time I got home the bottom of the bag was all wet and some of the messages had fallen out. Mum looked at me and asked, 'Where's the rest of the shopping, Paddy, and what happened to the bleach?'

Mum had some male friends who would come round to see her now and again. One in particular we called Uncle Ernie. He wasn't my idea of an uncle, and he didn't have time for us. I didn't like him: he was never nice to us and never played with us. He picked on us for any small reason he could think of. When Mum and

Uncle Ernie wanted to be alone together my brothers and sister would get up really early and stand outside on the landing while they did what they did on the other side of the closed door.

We always looked forward to Christmas and getting our bright red stockings, which would be full of chocolate coins, nuts and oranges. One Christmas I got a bright red Post Office letter box savings bank, some cardboard money and a set of bright red scales which I remember playing with for hours. Sometimes when times were very hard, though, we would have to share stockings. Once Brian found Mum sitting on the bed crying because she couldn't afford to put big presents in our stockings.

'How am I going to put smiles on all your faces?' she asked him.

Brian put his arm around her and said, 'Don't cry, Mum. It doesn't matter as long as we are all together.' I think even he was quite surprised at how grown up he sounded.

Mum's health was getting worse now. She was smoking a lot in those days; Woodbines were her ciggies of choice. She had a really nasty cough and she would vomit violently into a bucket, which we kept under the table. Her suffering used to tear me up inside, especially when she leapt out of bed in the middle of the night and dived for the bucket. I thought I would be sick myself just watching her retching her insides out. Every day one of us would go to the toilet on the landing to empty the bucket and wash it out, just in case we had visitors.

Two days after my seventh birthday, on 20

19

March 1958, I was out playing in the street when I saw this creamy white ambulance pull up outside our house. I'd been in one before when Mum had taken me to hospital though I don't remember what was wrong with me. I stood watching to see where the ambulance men were going. They stopped outside our flat and then disappeared through the front door. I wanted to go upstairs after them but I just stood there waiting to see who they were going to bring out. A few more kids had gathered outside by the ambulance by this time. I waited and waited. Eventually the front door opened and the ambulance men appeared carrying a stretcher. And at one end of it, poking out of the crumpled bright red blanket, was my Mum's drawn, pale face, her hair neatly combed.

As they approached the ambulance I ran towards Mum. I was frightened and beginning to panic. She raised her frail head slightly and told me to come closer. I didn't speak.

'It's all right, son. I'm just going away for a little while to get better. You be a good boy for your brothers and sister, promise me. I love you.'

Then she was half-tilted into the ambulance and disappeared from my sight as the doors closed. I just stood there thinking about what she had just said to me. The ambulance slowly pulled away from the kerb and made its way to the top of the street. As it turned left I started to run after it, but it just got further and further away until it disappeared for good — just like my mum behind those doors. I turned round slowly and started to walk back to the house. I couldn't stop the tears streaming down my face. I could still hear Mum's words ringing in my ears: 'Be a good boy . . . I love you.'

2

When I got back to the house, Auntie Pat was explaining to Claudy and Brian what was going to happen next. She said that some people were coming and they would make sure we were taken care of. She helped us get some of our things together and then we sat on the bed and waited. A man and a woman eventually arrived and the man asked us if we would like to go for a ride in the taxi to a new home, just until Mum got better. We all piled into the waiting taxi and I stared out of the dark rear window as it drove away from the house.

The taxi meandered along streets and roads I'd never seen or heard of, finally stopping at a tree-lined avenue of cottages. We were met by a woman who ushered us into a big room and then left, locking the door. She didn't say one word to us, just turned and locked the door behind her. We had never been locked in a room before and didn't know what to do, but there were toys scattered around so we played with them until she came back into the room and told us in no uncertain terms not to, and again locked the door behind her. We spent the rest of the day there until the other kids came back from school, and then we were allowed to join them for tea.

We spent about a week in this cottage before the same man and woman bundled us into another taxi and took us to a place called

Woolton, a well-to-do area. Although it seemed a million miles from Liverpool 8, it was actually a suburb in the south of the city. The houses were large and detached, not packed together like those where we lived, and there was so much space and it was so green. The taxi stopped outside a Georgian building set back off the road and hidden among the trees and foliage. A winding path led to the front porch and entrance: this was St Catherine's Convent, otherwise known as Druid's Cross. If anyone asked us where we lived, we'd tell them Druid's Cross.

On arrival we were greeted at the door by a very strange-looking woman dressed in a long black robe and a massive white hat on her head, which looked like a giant butterfly. She took us into a huge hallway, whose silence was broken only by the gentle tick-tocking of the big grandfather clock standing proudly by the visitors' waiting room. Directly in front of us was a giant crucifix with a figure of Jesus hanging on it, blood oozing from his forehead and from his hands, which were nailed to the cross, and a gaping wound in his side. It was very lifelike and a bit frightening. It reminded me of the time I'd wandered inside a church, but at least then I'd had my own guns! I'd been out playing in the streets with them and was wearing my Hopalong Cassidy hat. I saw this big house and thought I'd pretend I was busting my way into a saloon. A man gently told me that if I cared to leave my guns on the back pew I was welcome to look around.

We were then taken around various parts of the convent and introduced to other women dressed like the first one. We were handed new clothes, given baths and finally shown to our dormitories. Claudy was taken separately to the girls' one. Mum was still on my mind and questions kept running through my head. When were we going to see her again? How long was she going to be in hospital? When could we see her? Where was Paul?

A week or so later, at dinnertime, we were all sitting at our tables in the canteen waiting for the head sister to serve out the food. It was liver, potatoes, vegetables and gravy. After grace had been said, everyone began to tuck in and the general din of children eating, knives and forks being scraped against plates or dropped on the floor, and dinner trolleys squeaking as they were manoeuvred between the tables began to dominate, only to be broken by the barking of one of the nuns ordering Brian to eat his liver. Brian said he didn't like liver and refused to eat it. When he refused a second time she grabbed him by the hair, pulled him out of his chair and dragged him to the entrance of the canteen. Brian started to struggle to get free so she hit him all over his body. She even hit him in the face and made his nose bleed. And as if her hands couldn't do enough damage, she hit him with the gravy ladle as well while he lay helpless on the floor. Us kids weren't sitting together and I watched in horror and fear. We had never encountered physical violence before. I couldn't see Claudy or Michael's faces but I could imagine they felt the same way. Then, as if that wasn't enough, the sister ordered Brian to wait outside until Mr Glenn, who was in charge of the boys, arrived, whereupon he was pulled into the corridor and given another beating.

I didn't know about Jesus or sin, or what was right and what was wrong, but this felt very wrong. This unfamiliar environment terrified me. The happiness in the belief that one day we would all be together as soon as Mum was better was short-lived.

Of course, Brian wasn't the only one to suffer at the hands of Attila the Nun; there would be many more times when either I or one of the other kids would be beaten with a wooden coat hanger or caned for some childish misdemeanour. She could deliver a good right hook too.

Most of the kids attended St Mary's, the Roman Catholic school in Woolton, which was about three doors away from the Archbishop of Liverpool's official residence. We wore grey trousers, a white shirt, blue blazer and a cap. The school had an almost Gothic look to it yet was quite friendly, and we set off in pairs for the short walk from the convent. I was still missing Mum but now school was beginning to occupy my thoughts as well.

On the nights when we used to hang outside the pub waiting for Mum, sometimes it would be raining heavily or there might be thunder and lightning, but I was never afraid. I knew Mum was nearby and that I was with my brothers and sister. In fact, I found it quite exciting. A flash would light up the whole street followed by the loudest rolling, cracking thunder you ever heard. I loved it — that is, until we arrived at this place and it became something to be frightened of. The nuns told me one day that my sins had been found out and God was angry with me, and that my soul would burn forever in the depths of hell. I thought he must be very angry and maybe he was throwing furniture about the skies in a violent rage. From that day on I was afraid and I started bed-wetting, giving the nuns another reason to punish me.

In the mornings the 'wet beds' — Michael and me mainly, but there were a few other kids — would have to stand in the corridor by the stairs leading to the girls' dormitories so that they could see us with our wet sheets unceremoniously draped over our heads as they went down to breakfast. Then we were made to have cold baths before we could join everyone else. Sometimes I was sent to school with no socks, another form of punishment, I suppose, but I can't remember. On another occasion Michael and I were told to go and see the sister in the sewing room where she was just putting the finishing touches to a couple of pairs of rubber pants. She told us to take off our trousers and put the pants on. Then she grabbed us by the hand and dragged us to the girls' playroom where once again we were paraded in front of all the giggling girls. All we could do was stand there as tears streamed down our faces.

Every Saturday all the boys would be taken to the swimming baths on Queen's Drive. One particular Saturday one of the nuns took us. We would get the bus there and come back on foot. On the way back I desperately wanted to go to the toilet and asked the nun if it would be OK if I went in a nearby alleyway. She refused and ordered me to keep walking. I pleaded with her again but still she refused. I couldn't hold it in any longer and wet myself. When we arrived back at the convent I was told to go and see Mr Glenn up in the far room, so called because it was at the end of a long corridor. He ordered me to drop my trousers and then lie across his knee. I started crying before he even brought his hand thrashing down on my behind, and I was still crying when I pulled my trousers up. He looked at me and said, 'I haven't finished yet', and told me to take my trousers down again. He started to thrash me again. It felt like an eternity.

★   ★   ★

Time went by and there was still no news about Mum, and over the long months people came and went. Sunday visiting days were my loneliest, when the other kids would have family visits and go for walks to the park and get sweets, toys, books and crayons. I longed for the day when Mum would come and see us.

One Sunday afternoon we were just about to go to benediction and afternoon prayers in the chapel. We had all assembled in pairs by the door of our playroom, having gone through Mr Glenn's ritual procedure. Before we went anywhere we would have to stand in a line facing him, an arm's length apart from each other, and call out our individual number — 'One, two, three . . . ' — and then do it again in reverse. Mr Glenn ran us as if the whole thing was a military operation. Anyway, my mind was anywhere but the chapel when I felt a tap on my shoulder. I turned around and my eldest brother Paul was standing there. He told Michael and me to come with him. I couldn't believe he was here and jumped all over him and asked where Mum was. He smiled and pointed to the visitors' room, the door of which which was slightly open. I walked quickly towards the door and pushed it further open. Brian and Claudy were already inside, and then I caught sight of Mum. I flung the door wide open, ran over to her and dived into her arms. All the pain, anguish and loneliness were gone in an instant. I was happy, and, although we were in a convent and not at home, we were all together again. I had my family back at last.

We all wanted to kiss and hug Mum and smothered her and bombarded her with questions. 'Are you well now, Mum?' 'Are we going home now?' 'Why can't we go home with you now?' 'But you are getting better, aren't you, Mum?' Needless to say, Mum couldn't get a word in edgeways. She came with us to chapel and sat on the left-hand side with Claudy and the other girls. Paul sat with Brian, Michael and myself on the opposite side. I didn't like going to chapel as an hour of prayer for me was a wasted hour of playing time, and it was particularly being wasted as Mum was here. I was just itching to get out of there and down the road to the park with Mum. I kept my eyes glued on her and, once we got to the park, I only let go of her hand when I went to play. I kept looking over my shoulder, making sure she was still there. There was a theatre in the park and every Sunday there would be entertainment, singsongs and talent contests, and on this particular day Mum was with us I got up on stage along with some other kids.

It was the happiest day of my life. When the time came for Paul and Mum to leave I wanted to go with them. We all wanted to go back with Mum but it was not possible and, just like the day the ambulance pulled away from 82 Upper Canning Street, I ran down the long driveway leading to the main road waving and shouting to Mum not to forget to come next week. The next seven days couldn't pass too quickly for me; my mind was focused only on the following Sunday.

When Sunday did finally come round, we were waiting by the main gate watching all the other visitors arriving. I kept running up and down the driveway to see if Mum and Paul were in sight, saying to myself over and over again, 'Mum's definitely coming. She promised us. I know they are coming.' It was fixed firmly in my head and nothing was going to change it. As the afternoon wore on I tried not to give up hope even as the parents we had watched arrive now began to leave. She said she would come. Why didn't she come? She never came, not that Sunday, not the following Sunday, nor the one after that.

Then one day we were all called into the sister superior's office and told that our mum had died. I just stood there, unable to speak or move. Claudy burst into tears. Brian put his arms around all of us. Somehow I couldn't show any immediate emotion. It was as if I had been struck dumb and numb. I pulled myself away from Brian's arms and wandered off to the grounds around the convent and found myself a quiet spot, sat down and stared silently into space. I couldn't cry. I just couldn't accept it and I kept wanting to go back into the sister superior's office and tell her she had got it wrong, that my mum wasn't dead, that she would be back here next week to see us. There must be some mistake, I kept telling myself. It's got to be someone else's mother, not ours. None of us went to Mum's funeral and we were not told where she had been buried. It finally sunk in six months later that Mum was never coming back.

3

Every year, a few weeks before Christmas, the convent put on a pantomime for the benefit of the parents and important visitors. This year it was *The Pyjama Game*. I was cast as a robber who breaks into this house while all the occupants are watching telly in the living room and steals the silverware.

I was excited at the thought of being on stage and performing in front of strangers. I had previously been thrown out of the school band for excessive use of the drums. I had been determined to have the last word, so to speak, at the end of every song, and, not wanting to be outdone by the ting of a triangle or some other instrument, I would drown out the young musician with a rapid flurry on the drums.

'What's a foster parent,' I asked our Michael as we waited in the wings dressed only in our pyjamas, ready to make our first entrance.

'I think they are people who pretend to be your mum and dad if you haven't got any of your own,' said Michael.

'Would we have to call her Mum?' I asked. 'Does that mean we get to leave here? Go and live in a big house? Will we be going to a new school? Are we all going together?' He just grinned and nodded. He too was excited at the prospect of getting out of this place and leaving the past eighteen months or so behind him.

31

We peeked through the curtains into a sea of faces and wondered who had come to see us. We soon found out after the play was over when we were introduced to a fat lady called Mrs Grant and her daughter and son-in-law.

'You were all very good. I can see you being an actor when you grow up,' she said with a broad grin, addressing the last to me. 'My name is Mary and we have a big house and you'll go to a new school and make new friends. We have a car so we'll be able to go out on day trips and go on holiday.' She told us that she already had four other foster sons living with her and that they were all brothers.

'So, would you like to come and live with us?'

I looked at this large lady and imagined her big house, hoping it would be like the ones I had seen in my *Janet and John* books: a cosy family, Mummy and Daddy and Tip the dog, all standing by the front gate, flowers on either side of the path leading up to the front door, a blue sky and the sun shining down. In reality, it was a boarding house from hell.

Mary had three daughters, Beth, Fran and Jane and one son named David. Her husband was known as Pop; he was a quiet man, always smiling. Fran, who was the eldest daughter, was married to a retired policeman. She was the first woman I ever knew who could drive a car and I thought, wow, she must be really brainy. She had a black Ford Anglia and she was the one who picked us up from the convent.

Mary's home was really like a boarding house, lots of rooms and a toilet on each landing. She told us that there were a lot of lodgers staying at the house and that most of them were at work. The youngest of the brothers was our age and was waiting in the front room to meet us. He was about the same age as Michael and his complexion was a shade darker than ours. He had a toffee apple in one hand.

'This is one of your new brothers,' Mary said. 'His name is Ben.'

There was an awkward silence between us for what seemed like an age, then Ben held out his hand, the sticky one, challenging me to shake it. I gripped it and his face broke into a broad grin. Mary then told us to go out and play before dinner. Ben was the first to say anything. I think he was speaking to all of us but he seemed to be looking straight at me.

'Do you want to come and see a dead body?'

I didn't know what to say. A dead body! That's not exactly going out to play, is it? I wanted to say out loud, but I was in unknown territory here so I thought I'd better go along with whatever Ben wanted to do. Mary had given us some money to buy sweets but for some unknown reason we bought torches. We made our way up to the top of the road and then turned left on to the high street, which was very long and bustling with life. Ben was not too tall and not too small; he was podgy. I knew that one day I would be bigger than him, but now he had it over me, just.

We turned into a side street and stopped at a house midway down and Ben knocked on the door. I was feeling a little nervous, standing outside a stranger's house, not knowing what we were meant to say or do. Ben gave me a look that said relax, nothing's going to happen, and then the door opened. A palefaced lady stood there. Ben spoke first again.

'Hello, we are friends of your late son's friend and we would like to come in and pay our respects.'

Late son's friend. How could that be? This was our first day in the area and the only person I knew there and then was Ben.

The lady smiled and ushered us into the front parlour and there, laid out before us, was a coffin. It was open and inside lay the body of a young boy dressed in a sky-blue satin robe. I edged nearer to get a closer look. I stood there not quite knowing what to do or say. Ben then leant over and whispered in my ear, suggesting we say a little prayer before saying our goodbyes to the grieving lady sitting quietly in the back room. She smiled and thanked us for coming. On our way back to the house I asked Ben how the boy had died.

'He drowned in the swimming pool. He dived in at the shallow end and hit his head on the bottom. He never regained consciousness.'

I didn't know how to swim yet, so the thought of that young boy maybe two or three years older than me losing his life like that gave me a sinking, sickly, heavy feeling inside. I also thought: Thanks, Ben, for making this our first outing together. That was a barrel of laughs. What would he think of next time!

At Mary's we were allowed to have a bath twice a week. One day she came into the bathroom holding a full bottle of bleach, and started to pour it into the bath, telling us that it was harmless and that it would help us to get white and blend in with all the other kids. We believed her.

When we first moved to Mary's, she had one of those old prewar kitchen sinks, but about three months after our arrival it was replaced with a brand new stainless steel unit. Apart from social services providing money for our foster care, Mary was also getting rent from the lodgers. New things were arriving all the time — a television, telephone and new linoleum for the kitchen floor.

Our first Christmas at Mary's was memorable not least because brother Paul came to visit us. He arrived in the evening when it was party time in the front room. Mary had got Michael and me to blacken our faces with soot from the fireplace and sing songs that she was trying to teach us in front of her relatives. Michael and me were happy that we were making everyone laugh. When Paul saw us he thought it was anything but funny. He got some paper napkins and told us to wipe our faces clean. Michael and I looked at each other in confusion. We were too young to see that the joke was at our expense.

'What do you think you're doing?' he shouted at Mary. 'You ought to be ashamed of yourself. I know what your little game is, and I know about the bleach. I'm going to report you to the authorities. One minute you're trying to make them white and the next you're blackening them up. You don't deserve to foster children.'

Mary's face and neck turned scarlet, and the room went silent. Then she said, 'How dare you talk to me like that? It's just a bit of harmless fun. What I do in my house is no business of yours. Get out and don't come back.'

Paul didn't answer her. He just came over to us and said good-bye and told us he'd see us again, and not to worry for now.

Things didn't get better even though Michael and me were always eager to please. Mary would always say, 'Who wants to volunteer to do the dishes?'

'Me, me,' we'd shout in unison, putting our hands up in the air. When we didn't automatically volunteer, she would look displeased and say we were obviously tired and send us straight to bed. Soon the question became an order.

When one of Mary's daughters got married we were not allowed to travel in the cars with the family, instead we had to make our own way to the church on foot. Back at the house after the service we were told to stay outside while all the other guests enjoyed themselves inside. That's when I knew that we were not really part of that family and that we really didn't belong.

4

Our new school, St Sebastian's, was roughly a mile away from the house, and stood alongside the church of the same name, but set back off the road and situated slap in the middle of two playgrounds. Apart from feeling isolated within the family I also felt alienated at school not only because we were foster kids but because, apart from two others, we were the only black kids there. It was exhausting trying to explain my colour and my circumstances to my new classmates. I had to try and explain to them not just what an orphan was, but what a foster parent was as well, and then convince them that I was not born in Africa but in Liverpool 8, which was only two boroughs away.

'No, where are you really from?' they'd ask.

'I'm from Liverpool 8,' I'd repeat.

'No, where were you *born*?' they'd ask.

'I was born in Liverpool 8,' I'd reply.

Even the teacher would want to know where I was *really* from.

'Shall we look at the map on the wall, children, and see where Patrick's father might have come from?'

I made a few friends at school, among them the twins Barney and Danny Kelly, and Ian Cameron, but my first real friend was Paul Giles, who was very thin and very small, and the only one who invited me to his home. His dad had died recently and I had lost Mum only seven months earlier.

I first heard about his father's death in the classroom when the teacher was calling out the register. When Paul's surname was called out, one of the twins shouted out, 'Away, Miss'.

'Do you know why he is absent, Kelly?'

'His father died last night, Miss.'

At which point Miss Clark said, 'Oh, I'm very sorry to hear that. How did you learn about this, Kelly?'

'Our dads worked together, Miss.'

Amidst all the murmuring of the class, Miss Clark raised her voice and said, 'Quieten down now. I'm sure Paul will miss his father very much. Let us all bow our heads together now and say a silent prayer for Paul and the rest of his family.'

It was this shared sense of loss that cemented our friendship. We have remained close friends ever since.

★   ★   ★

Music always played a big part in my growing years. Buddy Holly, the Big Bopper, Paul Anka and, of course, Elvis, all contributed to my early appreciation of music and song. It was now the 1960s and with the sixties came a whole new generation of pop idols — Cliff Richard and the Shadows, Gene Pitney, Bobby Vee, Helen Shapiro, Marty Wilde, Adam Faith, Del Shannon. Their songs whirling around my head stopped me thinking about my miserable life.

Music would lift me up and transport me away from the real world, and what was going on around me. Claudy and her friends, the sisters of Barney and Danny, were also into the music scene, pulling their hair out and screaming at anything in blue jeans and a leather jacket.

There was always music playing on the radio in the house. I couldn't afford to buy records at the time and what little pocket money we had wouldn't have stretched that far. But I remember one of Mary's daughter's had a boyfriend at one time who was serving in the air force and every time he came home on leave the two of them would spend hours together listening to the latest songs he had managed to record on his Grundig reel-to-reel tape recorder. A particular favourite was John Leyton singing 'Johnny Remember Me'. You could hear music playing everywhere, especially in the milk bars, cafés where primarily teenagers would hang out — teddy boys, arms around their 'Judys' — listening to the jukebox. Whenever I heard 'Johnny Remember Me', I used to think it was my mum up there 'singing in the sighing of the wind . . . remember me'.

Another song that got a lot of airplay was 'Big Bad John', by Jimmy Dean, about a big man — 'He stood six foot two and weighed forty-five', who worked down the mines and 'took no lip'. One day the mine caved in and Big John saved all the miners but lost his own life. The refrain of the song went 'Big John, Big John, Big Bad John'. Well, one day after school had finished and the four o'clock bell had gone, Paul,

39

the twins and I went to the playground. A large group of older boys were taunting and jeering someone. As we got nearer we saw that it was Ben who was on the receiving end of their poking and prodding and abusive racist remarks. We took it personally — what they were saying to Ben could also apply to us — and we laid into them immediately and Paul went to fetch his elder brother. Ben somehow managed to fight his way out of the scrabble, only to return with a rounders bat he'd found in the schools sports cupboard. The gang immediately backed off and we cheered Ben on as we saw the looks on their faces change from anger to fear. From the yard we could see the street, cars passing by in both directions. One car suddenly screeched to a halt right in the middle of the road and out jumped this enormous feller. He ran straight into the playground and up to Ben and snatched the bat out of his hand. He immediately turned on the gang and shouted, 'Come on, come on, who wants to be the first? Come on, ya yella bastards. Wot's the marra wid yez? Who wants to take *me* on?' No one did. A stranger had come from out of nowhere and rescued Ben. We never ever saw Ben's saviour again but we christened him Big John. When we mentioned the incident to Mary, all she could say was 'That's life; you're going to have to live with it', or words to that effect.

I can't say I was a fast learner; maybe that was because I spent most of the time in the classroom corner. I was always in trouble for fights of some sort, always being sent for the cane or being told to stand in the corner. One of the very first times I actually sat up and paid attention to what was going on was when they showed us a film about where cocoa and chocolate came from, all filmed in the West Indies and Africa. I used to go off into fantasy land thinking I'd rather be there than here. Come playtime I'd sneak out of the playground just like I had done at Windsor Street and go to the shops and pinch sweets. If I had a few pennies I would buy broken biscuits from the local Irwin's store. I would get back in time for the bell to ring and for lessons to resume.

5

Mary took us on holiday to Caernarvon in North Wales. We stayed on a farm in a little town called Trevor, surrounded by hills and fields. It was nice to get away from Liverpool and the neighbours for a few weeks. As she was the only girl, Claudy was allowed to bring her best schoolfriend, Betty Stanton. We had lots of fun, milking the cows, feeding the pigs and hay-stacking. We played in the barn next to the farmhouse, swinging on a rope tied to one of the rafters and dive-bombing into the freshly stacked bales of hay. Suddenly Claudy passed out right before our eyes. One minute we were laughing and fooling about, the next she was out like a light. We all thought she was joking.

'Come on, Claudy. Stop messing about. It's not funny any more,' I said.

Then Brian said, 'She's still not moving.'

Luckily the farmer was nearby and he held a brown bottle of smelling salts right under her nose, which woke her up immediately, to our relief.

From the farmhouse window, straight ahead in the distance, you could see a very big mountain, which looked like a giant tea cosy. One morning Michael and I could just make out Ben, Brian and David at the top of Mount Tea Cosy gesturing for us to join them at the top. As we made our way up Michael suddenly piped up,

'Hope yer keeping yer eye out for snakes.'

I stopped right in my tracks and said to him, 'That's it, I ain't going any further', and immediately started back down the mountain, leaving Michael to continue on his own. When they all returned to the farm later I was ribbed and teased about being afraid of snakes and doing a runner.

Even though we were far away from home we still didn't get far away from racist abuse. We came across some Welsh kids in the local village corner shop and they started calling us names so we beat the shite out of them. In fact, the Welsh kids turned out to be all right. They apologised to us a bit later on — 'We come to say we are very sorry for the things we shouted at you the other day, see, we were only having a laugh, see' — said it wouldn't happen again and hoped we would have a nice stay on the farm.

We didn't tell Mary but she found out anyway and made us feel as if we were the ones to blame, and that we had embarrassed her. She told us she would never take us on holiday again.

6

Right at the very beginning the nuns at St Catherine's had advised Mary that Mike and myself had bed-wetting problems and therefore needed proper bedlinen and waterproof mattresses. She ignored their advice and instead would just humiliate and scold us in front of the lodgers. Fear of punishment only made the problem worse. She did eventually get protective rubber sheets from the authorities, but skimped on the actual mattresses. She just placed the rubber sheets, which were sewn together, on top of the bed springs and made Michael and me sleep on the bed like that.

Then, one day when we got back from school, Mary announced she was going to put a stop to our bed-wetting once and for all. She told her eldest daughter to go and fetch the things. She returned with a roll of lino and the big kitchen scissors. Mary then told us to follow her upstairs to the bedroom.

'You two get undressed, stand there and don't move!' she ordered.

As we slowly started to undress I was thinking to myself, this is really happening. It's not a dream. I am awake and this is happening. We were both too scared to say anything — not that Michael ever did as he had a stutter, which was more pronounced when he was anxious or stressed. Whenever I did say something or question anything it was more than likely that I'd be hit.

When we were naked she told us to lie down on the floor. Mary then unrolled the lino and laid it next to us, cutting along the roll as if she was cutting Christmas paper.

'This is for your own good, you two. I'll soon cure you of your filthy habits.'

After she had measured and cut the linoleum we were told to stand up and hold our arms up in the air. She then wrapped the measured piece around each of us, securing it with parcel tape. We were now encased in lino up to our armpits and unable to move. The only bits of our bodies left exposed were our feet, arms, head and shoulders. Fran then took hold of my feet while Mary grabbed me under the shoulders and together they lifted me on to the bed springs. I watched as they did the same with Michael. Next Mary produced small pieces of rope and proceeded to secure our hands to the sides of the bed frame. We were completely immobile and absolutely helpless. In the morning she would come into the room, untie us and send us off to school. This treatment went on for about two weeks and all we could do was stare at the ceiling as we slept fitfully, waking up every time we wanted to turn over or move.

We used to call Mary Mum. It felt strange at first because I knew she wasn't my mum and I never really got used to it. Her behaviour was anything but motherly.

I used to dread coming home from school and began to wonder seriously if any of the aunties or uncles — Uncle Tefra or Auntie Maize perhaps — would let me come and live with them. I used to dawdle coming home from school on purpose. I'd ask the teachers if I could stay behind and clean the blackboard, just so I had a perfect excuse for being late home from school, anything to stay out in the open for as long as I could. I couldn't bear the sight of Mary spitting into the range where we had to make the fire in the mornings and clean and polish the grate with the old zebrite, or the sound of her putting on a posh voice whenever she had visitors or when our welfare officer came by, as he did every six months. She was nice as pie to his face but would call him names behind his back.

Once, just before he was due to visit, she told us that 'Lord Connor' was coming to take us shopping to get new clothes for the autumn. I was excited and in the car on the way to T.J. Hughes, the big department store, I said to Mr Connor, 'Mum calls you Lord Connor.' He didn't say anything. After he had dropped us back home and left, Mary called me into the kitchen.

'Would you mind opening your mouth as wide as you can?' she said, looking at me in a questioning way.

'Do you want to know what I'd like to do with that?' she spat at me and swiftly brought her hand from behind her back and hit me on the side of my face with such force that I went reeling backwards across the kitchen floor.

'Don't you ever open your mouth in front of Mr Connor like that again.'

Then she ordered me to get out of her sight, something she was constantly telling me to do. Mary called the welfare officer Lord Connor because she thought he was above himself. In my innocence, I had embarrassed her and she wasn't going to let me get away with it.

She was cruel and vindictive to Brian and Claudy, too. Once we were outside playing. It was just around Easter and we were all given new clothes and Claudy had a lovely dress with flowers all over it. Mary saw Claudy halfway up the tree and called her indoors. And while Claudy was still wearing her dress she told her to turn around so that her back was towards her. She took hold of the bottom hem of her dress and gripped it at the seams and pulled them with such force the dress just came apart: reduced to tears, Claudy was sent back out to play in the ripped dress.

Chewing gum was not allowed anywhere in the house (or in the street, for that matter) as Mary thought that it was a disgusting habit, and one day she caught Brian out. She made him remove it from his mouth and hand it over to her. Then she grabbed him by the neck and started to rub the gum into his hair. The only way to remove it was with a razor blade and scissors, which left him with two large bald patches.

Outside and away from the house I was at peace with myself, and my mind was less troubled. As soon as I woke up I got out of the house. One day I was out playing on a piece of waste ground opposite pretending to be the

Lone Ranger. I was in the middle of a fight with one of my invisible enemies, Jake the Snake, who had ambushed me as I came through the pass. I was really having a good time, throwing myself on the ground and wiping my chin as though I had been caught with a left hook. I was so immersed in this fight with my invisible foe that I didn't realise I was being observed by Mary and her daughters until I heard them laughing at me and mocking me. They didn't think it was funny, just stupid. That was the end of my invisible friends and foes.

Another time I woke during the night to see Mary and two of her daughters standing over Michael and me, laughing. I realised that they were laughing at the way we rocked simultaneously in our sleep; this seemed to amuse them. Michael and I used to laugh with each other as a way of coping with our day-to-day misery. We would laugh at everything. One of Mary's daughters got into a row with our Claudy, Brian and Ben, and the angrier she got the more we giggled. We were all sitting around the kitchen table at the time and Mike and me had our backs to the kitchen wall so there was no escape when she threatened to throw a bowl of porridge at us. This just made us more hysterical. Well, we saw it coming and just parted so that it hit the wall behind us.

We were only allowed to come into the house by the back door; only visitors and friends of Mary's immediate family used the front entrance. The living room was strictly out of bounds to us and it was the only room with a television in it. Mary would let us in there every Monday night so that we could watch *Wagon Train*, but as soon as it was over it was back to the kitchen where we would sit around the table playing board games. If we wanted to watch TV at any other time we would go around the corner and sit on the wall outside a friend's house and peer through their window to watch their telly.

We even had our meals separately. The family and the lodgers had cooked meals every night, while we had four rounds of bread and butter each and a dollop of jam. That was our tea every day when we got home from school and that was all we ever had. Mary and her family didn't care about us; we were just a nice little earner for them. We were no more than paying guests and were never going to be part of the family.

When Mr Connor did come to visit us to see how we were settling in those early weeks, we didn't have much to complain about, and Mary hadn't begun to treat us badly yet. It was only as time went by that things deteriorated. Mary would be present most of the times he visited us, so we wouldn't say anything negative as we had grown more fearful of Mary and didn't know what she would do to retaliate. Many years later, when I was doing *The Brothers McGregor* at Granada, Mr Connor came to a studio recording of one of the episodes. I told him then of all the things that had happened at Mary's that we hadn't been able to tell him at the time.

7

One bright sunny day I was playing just outside the house when a car pulled up alongside me. The window was wound down and the man inside called me over. He was smiling and wanted to know where a certain road was. I walked over and pointed him in the direction he needed to go. Still smiling, he asked me if I would mind getting into the car and showing him exactly where it was. It was only a few streets away so I was happy to help knowing it would only take me a few minutes to walk back to my road. When we got there, he stopped the car and asked me if I could keep a secret. I said yes. Then he asked me if I would like to play with him. Again I said yes, wondering what game it would be. He turned and said to me, 'My willy is sore. Can you kiss it better for me?' He took his penis out and told me to make it better by stroking it and kissing it. He put his hand on the back of my head and lowered it down towards his lap. I wasn't scared and I didn't feel that I was doing anything wrong because all along he kept telling me that I was a good boy. Afterwards he told me again that I was a good boy. Then he started the car again and drove me back towards the place he had picked me up. As he stopped the car he shoved a two shilling piece into my hand, winked at me and said, 'Remember, this is our little secret, eh?' I had two shillings in my

50

hand and so I headed off to the sweetshop, not knowing that my childhood innocence had just been abused as well as my body.

As I neared home I met Brian and David and, just as we were about to go into the house they said in unison, 'You've had it, Paddy. We know about you and the man in the car. He told us all about it and what you did.'

When the police arrived I began to worry. It was then that I thought I had done something wrong and was in serious trouble. They asked me to describe all that I could about the man in the car and told me how important it was for them to find him. When the police had finished questioning me they told me again how brave I had been and that I wasn't to get into any other strangers' cars ever again. As a child you are brought up to believe that adults are a protective force and as an innocent eight-year-old boy I hadn't realised that what had happened earlier that day had been wrong. I couldn't understand why the man had broken 'our little secret' by telling my brothers. The police told me I was lucky to be alive and reassured me that it was not my fault, but Mary and the rest of her family treated me like an untouchable. They made me feel like it *was* my fault, that I was the instigator and that I wasn't to be trusted to go out on my own any more. As Mary put it, I was 'a dirty little boy'.

It seemed that the only adults who were nice to me were strangers. Often when I was out playing on my own I would go and watch the workmen resurfacing the main road where the

old disused tramlines were still visible. Sometimes I found the odd penny on the tramlines
that hadn't been done yet and I'd do odd jobs
for the navvies, who were very friendly.

'Hey, mister, can I get you some water? Do
you want any help? They would wink at me and
say, 'Of course, son, fetch that water barrel and
bring it over here', or they'd send me to the
shops to buy ciggies and let me keep the change.
Sometimes they would let me sit with them in
their little huts by the roadside and share their
sandwiches, and even, on the odd occasion, give
me the loose change from their wage packet.
More often than not it would be half a crown.

8

The day I ran away came as a surprise to me, and a shock to everyone else. It was a scorching hot summer's day and I had been playing outside close to the house when I ran in to get a glass of water. Mary came storming into the kitchen demanding to know who had removed the ladder that was supposed to be leaning up against the outside loo. I'd used it to climb on to the shed earlier that morning, though I denied being responsible this time because I couldn't take another clip or slap across the face. Pointless, because she still took a swipe at me, but I dodged her swing and ran out of the back door, slamming it behind me. She followed me out into the street and shouted at me to come back and shut the door properly. I turned to face her and said no.

'What did you say?'

'No,' I shouted back this time. I'd had enough and knew I'd get slapped again. I shouted back no. I could see that if I did go back she would take another swing at me. We stood there for a moment glaring at each other, her eyes filled with rage, mine with defiance.

'You get back here right now and close this door properly,' she hissed.

'No, no, no,' I yelled. Then I turned on my heels and started to run, though I had no idea where I was going. I just had to get away from her, away from the constant accusations and bashings. And school was no better. I got caned there for things I didn't think were my fault either — like fighting other kids because of some racist remark or having to write out lines because I had forgotten my gym shorts. The words 'See me afterwards' scrawled across my exercise book would fill me with dread. All these thoughts were rushing through my head as I ran up the street. I turned to look back and saw Mary pointing at me, and Eric, one of the lodgers, was kneeling down and fastening his shoelace, as though preparing for the Edge Hill Mile.

I had to make my mind up which direction I was going to take. To my left were Old Swan and Childwall (Liverpool suburbs), also my school route, and to my right Liverpool 8, and Upper Canning Street — my old home. I chose safety and sanctuary. Eric was now on his feet and running, and began to pull away from Mary like an old steam engine pulling out of Lime Street on a Bank Holiday Monday. Eric was never going to make it to the top of the road, but in order to save face in front of Mary he had to go for it. I let him get halfway up the road before I took off in the direction of Liverpool 8 and the chase was on.

Eric managed to follow me through the park but I lost him on the high street and headed off towards 'the Eight'. Turning into Tunnel Road, I could sense that I was almost there. I could now see the top of the big Anglican cathedral — my landmark; it would only be a matter of minutes before I would feel completely safe and at home.

The only thing for me to do now was to find one of my aunties, someone who would listen to me and tell me that I never had to go back to Mary's. Then I got to 82 Upper Canning Street, and, seeing it again after three years, it was as though nothing had changed. Everything — the houses and the people — seemed the same. I could rejoin this community right now, and know that I was part of it all; all I needed to do was to check in with an auntie, then I could go out and play. Auntie Pat had lived in the flat below us and I was desperately hoping that she would be there now. Memories came flooding back as I approached her front door, but that didn't make me sad. Mum had gone, I knew, but I also knew that if Auntie Pat would let me stay, and not make me go back to Westbank Road, then I would be happy again.

I knocked on the door not knowing what I was going to say to Auntie Pat or what her reaction would be. Her face appeared from behind the door and I started to cry.

'Auntie Pat, I've run away. I don't want to go back there. Will you let me stay with you? I don't like where we are. Please don't send me back, she will beat me.'

'I'm sorry, son, I can't let you stay with me, unless the authorities say you can, and I haven't got enough room for you all here. You must go back, Paddy, or you'll get in trouble.' She looked sad that she couldn't help me. She gave me a hug and some money to get back to Mary's and to buy some sweets.

I went to the sweetshop and Mrs Rimmer, the

same old lady with the white streak in her hair, was there. Memories of a Bonfire Night came flooding back. Mum had been happy that night and she had given us two half-crown pieces to go and buy sparklers, Catherine wheels, rockets and bangers.

'Please, can I have a lolly ice, four Walker's and a bubble gum?' I asked politely.

'Hello, son. I remember you,' she said, and my thoughts immediately sprang to the song by Frank Ifield — 'I remember you, you're the one who made my dreams come true' — transporting me back to Westbank Road. 'You're one of Margaret's boys, aren't you?'

'I'm Patrick,' I replied. 'I've run away from our foster parents. We all want to come back and live around here.'

'I'm sorry about your mum, son. She was a lovely woman and I'm sure you must miss her very much.' She curled my fingers around the money back into my palm and wished me luck. She had the same helpless but kindly look on her face as Auntie Pat as I said goodbye.

I wasn't going back to Mary's but instead made my way to Uncle Tefra's. When I got there I knocked twice and waited. No answer. I waited a little longer, standing on tiptoe to peer through the letter box. I then pressed my ear to the open flap, listening for the familiar sound of the radio. I sniffed the air for that rich flavoured tobacco smell that had so often hypnotised me when he had made us laugh.

The silence was louder than the noise on the pavement. The hallway looked empty, as if no one had been there for a few weeks, months maybe, but I kept knocking. I stood there for what seemed like ages until eventually a woman from across the road came over and asked me who I was looking for. I told her I had come to see my Uncle Tefra who lived here.

'Oh,' she said. 'He died a few weeks ago. There's no one living there any more, son. I'm sorry.'

I walked away, saddened. I wandered around my old haunts, checking that they were still there, retracing my old routes to school and where I would go after I had bunked off — the waste ground behind the Rialto, the old car dump just in front of the big Anglican cathedral, the cemetery, the big air vents on top of the flour mills at the bottom of Parley Street by the overhead railway, the Pier Head. I wandered round most of these places that afternoon, enjoying the warmth, enjoying the freedom, but I was still on the run and had to find somewhere to go, had to find another auntie.

I then made my way towards Granby Street, the busiest street in Liverpool 8. The place was just heaving with people of all colours and races — butchers, bakers, fruit and veg, sewing shops, knitting shops, pet shops; it even had a dairy farm. When I used to stay with Auntie Dolly some years earlier (I must have been three or four) I would hear the cocks crowing every morning, and although I couldn't actually see them it gave me a sense that the farms and countryside were just around the corner. Hatherley Street was actually just around the corner now and I approached it with a sense of urgency, quickening my pace. I crossed over from the sunny side of the street on to the shaded steps leading up to the door. I knocked and waited, looking down into the basement window for any signs of life. From outside I could see the old table in the middle of the room with its plastic floral tablecloth, sugar bowl, teapot, cup and saucer, three-quarter pint of milk, reading glasses and newspaper.

Peering through the letter box, I could see a familiar figure moving slowly but steadily towards the door. It was Auntie Dolly. The door opened and there she stood, looking down at me standing in the doorway. It must have been about five years since I'd lived with Auntie Dolly, but looking round the living room I could still see the big old Welsh dresser, adorned with the same fancy plates and teapots, the old bedlinen chest in the corner of the room, which was my bed, and opposite, on the other side of the room, the old radiogram just under the window. I knew from the way Auntie Dolly was moving that my chances of staying with her, and of her looking after me, were very slim, but I did manage to tell her about my unhappiness at Mary's. She wasn't as chatty and welcoming as Uncle Tefra would have been; it was almost as if she didn't want to talk about Mum. But she did talk about my father, this big dark merchant seaman who came to see me all the time, and who used to stay with her. He was a West African who would often turn up with presents and new clothes for me before disappearing again. Dolly shuffled over to the

Welsh dresser, opened one of the big cupboard doors below and produced a large biscuit tin. Removing the lid, she rummaged through old letters and documents before producing a photograph which she handed to me. It was a picture of me standing outside her front window against the railings, flanked by two very pretty white girls who were two or three years older than I was. It was the very first time I had ever seen a picture of myself that young and I had never seen me looking so happy. There was very little to say to Auntie Dolly during my visit. A sense of hopelessness came over me as she too explained that, sooner or later, I would have to go back to Mary's, but she did say that if we all stuck together the authorities would have to do something about it. When we got to the top of the stairs she turned to me, gave me a hug and told me to look after the photo she had given me. Then she opened the door and once more I stepped out into the street, immediately crossing over the road to the sunny side.

The sun was sinking as the afternoon wore on. I still hadn't found my safe haven and was already thinking about having to go back, but, as it was still light, I made my mind up that I wasn't going to go back till it was dark. As long as I was out in the open I felt safe; there still seemed to be hope. I kept looking at the picture Auntie Dolly had given me. From the big, broad grin on my face it was clear to me that I'd been a happy boy, now here I was, a fugitive, on the run. I had to start planning how I was going to get back into the house. I knew the front door would be open and thought that perhaps I could sneak in and go straight to bed. I thought that the later I got back the less chance she had of hitting me and making me scream for my life. If I could just get back there and sneak into bed and then get up and off to school first thing, she'd miss out altogether on the chance to belt me. And then it suddenly occurred to me that the next morning was Sunday. Well, what could possibly happen to me on a Sunday morning? My heart began pounding as I made my slow way out of Liverpool 8 and into Liverpool 7.

The sun had gone down by now, the streets were emptying and lights were coming on all around me. I approached the house and stood outside under the kitchen window. I could hear my brothers and sisters talking. Then I moved a few paces and stood under Mary's window. The television was on and I couldn't make out if she was in the room or if she was out somewhere looking for me. I went round to the front door, which we weren't normally allowed to use; it was open so I sneaked in past Mary's room and up the stairs to my bed and tried to get some sleep before anyone came up. I thought that if they saw me asleep they would not disturb me till the morning. But I couldn't sleep: my heart was thumping and my stomach was churning. At this time Michael and me were sharing a room with Eric, the permanent lodger who had chased me earlier in the day. So when Eric came up to bed and turned the light on, I thought this was it, this was the end of the world. This was going to be worse than the cellar treatment.

The cellar treatment was another of Mary's ways of stopping me from wetting the bed. Michael as well but mainly me because I suppose she saw me as the youngest and the most rebellious. Anyway, one time she locked me in the cellar and I was there for a whole hour before Pop, her husband, came and unlocked the door and put on the light at the top of the stairs. I knew where the switch was but I was too stiff and frightened and speechless to do anything. If it hadn't been for him, I would have spent the whole night locked in the cellar with the rats. I liked Pop and he liked us, and Mary resented this and him even more because he often took our side. We never saw much of him because he was always up early and out to work — he worked at the sausage factory — and I don't think he and Mary saw eye to eye. He didn't seem to have much to do with the running of the house: he just let Mary get on with it.

So there I was now, lying in bed with a flimsy blanket pulled over my head, with tiny specks of light creeping through the small holes in the blanket, listening to Eric gleefully telling me how I was in for the thrashing of my life. But one thing made me feel good in all this, and that was the photo I had of myself that Auntie Dolly had given me. I had it tucked safely under my pillow and I promised myself that I would treasure it for the rest of my life.

I awoke the next morning with a heavy, sick feeling inside me. My brothers and sister were anxious to know which aunties I had been to see and what it was like being back in 'the Eight', if only for a day. I was telling them about my day and showing them the picture that Auntie Dolly had given me when Mary walked in and ordered them all to leave the room. She then told me to go and wait for her in the front playroom. She came in and locked the door behind her and ordered me to strip off every item of clothing I was wearing. Then she picked up my clothes, unlocked the door and left, locking the door again behind her. She returned a few moments later carrying a cane. I still had the photo in my hand when she came towards me and snatched it from me. She looked at me, then at the picture and then back at me, as she held it up for me to see, with a cruel grin she tore the photograph into shreds, laughing as the tears started to roll down my face. The one good thing that had brought a smile to my face after my hopeless attempt to escape was now torn into tiny pieces and stuffed into her paisley patterned pinafore pocket. I screamed and ran towards her, knowing full well I was never going to get the better of her. But I thought, what the hell? I had nothing to lose. Although I had my memories of Liverpool 8 and the happy times before Mum died, she had just destroyed the proof. I went for her, and she laid into me with the cane and didn't stop until I was crouched in the corner of the room begging for mercy. She struck every part of my body until I was a crawling whelp.

'That's your breakfast,' she said and left the room, locking the door once more behind her. For the next few hours I lay motionless in the corner. I heard my brothers and sister returning from eleven o'clock mass and could soon smell breakfast. I thought of them eating bacon and eggs. Claudette sneaked up to the locked door and asked me if I was all right, and she pushed a couple of slices of bread under the door. I told her that I was OK and that as soon as I got some clothes on I'd be off again. I could hear Brian on the other side with Claudette telling me to be careful. Then it fell silent.

Soon I was disturbed by the sound of the key in the door and immediately my heart began to pound; my stomach felt as if I had just swallowed an anvil. I tried to push myself to an upright position, pressing my back and arms against the wall. Mary stood in the doorway, with her hands behind her back, as if daring me to try and get past her. Then she locked the door.

'Are you hungry?' she asked.

'Yes,' I said.

'Then here's dinner.' And she laid into me once more with the cane. I didn't think it could be any more painful than the first beating, but it was because she was slicing into my already sore and bruised skin. All because I had refused to go back and close a door properly behind me.

Finally, in the evening, I was allowed out of the room, given a blanket and told I would get my clothes back in the morning. I went into the kitchen and the looks on my brothers' and sister's faces when they saw my beaten body told us all that things couldn't go on like this, and that we'd have to look out for each other more in future.

It was a few days later that Brian got into

trouble with Mary, and this time we all decided to leave together and go back to Auntie Pat's. Our Michael had been sent to the shops to get the eight loaves of bread for our tea and for the lodgers and family's sandwiches, so we waited for him outside. As we saw him coming, arms outstretched like a fork-lift with eight loaves stacked neatly as if on a palette between them, we told him that we were all running away and he should go and drop off the loaves and then come and meet us at the end of the street. We waited for a bit but he didn't appear. We weren't going to go back so off we headed for 'the Eight' and to decide what to do when we got to Auntie Pat's. Claudette and Brian told her all the bad things that had been happening to us, and this time she knew she couldn't send us back. She sent me out to get some sweets and I had a spring in my step as I walked to the shop. I thought: This is it. We'll never have to go back. Things will get better now and soon I'll be back playing in my old haunts. Everything was going to be all right.

But as I turned into Upper Canning Street I was stopped dead in my tracks. My stomach suddenly felt heavy and my heart began to pound. There, parked outside the house, was Fran's green van. I dropped the sweets and ran towards the house. Mary's granddaughter leant out of the window and shouted, 'You've been a naughty boy, Paddy, you're in trouble.' As I climbed the stairs I could hear Mary and Auntie Pat talking in raised voices. No sooner had I reached the landing than I was turned straight around and led back downstairs, with Brian and Claudy, by Jimmy, Ben's older brother. We drove back to Westbank Road in silence and were told to wait in the front room. But this time the door wasn't locked. Michael was already in there and he told us that our welly was on the way. We heard the Liverpool Education minibus pull up outside and then heard Mary tell Mr Connor that we were now his responsibility and that she didn't want anything more to do with us. I was filled with real excitement: I was finally getting away from this place. I hadn't a clue where we were going but I didn't care. Mary came to the door to say that one or two of us could always come back and visit, but, looking me straight in the eye she said, 'You, Paddy Barber. I never want to see you here ever again.'

'OK,' I said and went to the van and we slowly pulled away. I took one last look behind me then turned, looked at my sister and brothers, and smiled.

9

As the minibus turned into Allerton Road I got the impression that we were going somewhere nice. We were now entering picture-postcard territory. We pulled up outside a Gothic-style mansion and were introduced to Mr and Mrs Kidd who were stood in the porch waiting to greet us, along with other members of staff. This place was called New Heys and it was an assessment centre as well as being a reception centre, which meant that we had to stay there for at least six months before they found us another children's home or a foster home.

We were introduced to the other kids and then kitted out with new clothes. They weren't anything like uniforms as such and they were all individual — Ladybird sweatshirts and jeans, sandals and shoes, etc. Somehow I was glad to get out of the clothes we had been wearing at Westbank Road. It felt good to start all over again and see what the future held in store for us now.

The next thing we were shown to our dormitories. Claudette, as usual, was directed to the girls' dorm which was on the top floor of the annexe across the yard from the main house. The boys' dorms, however, were all in the main house and differentiated by colour — blue, pink and green. The room they put Brian and me in was pink, and our Mike was put in the green dorm.

There were all sorts of kids there — kids who had been abandoned, some who had been abused, kids who had run away from their own homes and kids whose parents had died, like ours.

As usual, settling in the new home and making new friends was a routine formality. That evening when the lights had gone out we started whispering, then gradually we got louder until we were interrupted by the sound of Mr Kidd's voice bellowing from the bottom of the stairs, 'Threepence off the pink room.' It was only our first night and we had already lost a third of our pocket money. In the six months we were there we lost many more pennies, but we didn't mind because the staff and Mr Kidd were all very friendly and we were still left with a lot more than we had been getting at Mary's.

It was now the end of the summer holidays and the leaves were all but dropping to the ground. We should have been starting our autumn term at our new school, Cardinal Newman, but we had to attend the school which was adjacent to the home at New Heys. At first I was a bit concerned that I wouldn't be able to see my friend, Paul, the twins and Ian. I was hoping that our new home would be just like the one we were in now. We did lots of practical work in the school — making plaster moulds of animals, cats and the like, and making Christmas cards to send to our friends and decorations for the tree.

At one point we were each given a piece of toilet paper and a pencil and asked to write down what we most wanted for Christmas, our first and second choices. I asked for an Everton football kit, although it was more to do with the colour than the team. When Christmas morning came, we all opened our presents and I had got my Everton kit as well as the pair of boxing gloves I had asked for. After the Christmas holidays we were eventually allowed to go Cardinal Newman school and I was able to meet up with my old schoolfriends. When I realised that most of the kids in my class had asked for Liverpool football kits from their parents I soon found I was the only one in the class with a blue kit. I felt a right plank. Within a matter of weeks I went from being an Everton fan to the staunch Liverpool fan I am today.

We were allowed out on Saturdays to visit friends and to go swimming or to the pictures, and the general feel of the place was relaxed and friendly. Even the cook, who was short and portly, loved all the kids who invaded her kitchen, which was her domain. She had time for everyone and would even let you help out if you wanted to. There was never any pressure, not like at the other place. Many a time kids, including myself, would emerge from the kitchen with cream on our faces after we had scooped out the remains of the custard or anything sweet and sticky with our fingers.

I had my eleventh birthday in New Heys and remember trying to trick the staff that it was on St Patrick's Day — 17 March — just so that I would get extra pressies and extra special attention. They sussed me out but gave me more presents anyway.

Our time at New Heys was a world away from Mary's and we were no longer living in fear of being beaten every day. That's not to say we weren't punished. Brian got into an argument with a female member of staff and ended up hitting her. This didn't go down well with Mr Kidd who thrashed him with the cane.

We were allowed to go to the swimming baths in Garston every Saturday afternoon and it was here that I taught myself to swim. I had never forgotten the time, when we'd first gone to Mary's, that Ben took me to see the body of the boy who had drowned. I used to stand in the shallow end of the pool and slowly but steadily ease myself away from the bars and then make as if to dive at the bar. Every time I did it I would back further and further into the deep end and then scramble to the bar, splashing my arms about frantically. At the end of the session the pool attendant would blow his whistle and we would all immediately climb out of the pool and then run like mad to the other end and dive in again. This infuriated the attendant because it meant he would have to get the hose out to stop us doing the same thing again. One day Ben was running along the side of the pool when the attendant aimed the hose at his feet and the force of the jet made him stumble, fall and catch one of his front teeth on the edge of the pool. He lost half of it.

Michael and I were still bed-wetting, but not as frequently now, and at New Heys it was dealt with kindly and we were not singled out and punished for it. We were provided with rubber sheets and, if we did wet the bed during the night, in the morning all you had to do was take the wet sheet and put it in a large bath in a room beside the bathroom. Being in New Heys was a far better time for me and my sister and brothers, but it was a short-lived stay.

One day I was playing with my toys in the dormitory when Mr Kidd came in and sat down on my bed.

'So, Paddy, how are you? Are you happy here?'

'Yes, Mr Kidd,' I replied.

'You like all your brothers and your sister, don't you?'

'Yes, Mr Kidd, I like them very much.'

'I know you do, son, but supposing one day you had to leave here. Would you be sad?'

'Yes, Mr Kidd, I would be very sad 'cos all the staff are very nice and kind to us.'

'That's nice, Paddy, but you know one day you're going to have to leave us, don't you?' He paused and then said, 'Tell me something, Paddy. Out of all your brothers and sister, who's your favourite? Who do you like best?'

I told him that I liked them all. I lowered my eyes and stared at my toy gun. I wasn't quite sure what he was getting at with his questions.

'Brian's your big brother, isn't he? You like him a lot, don't you? I know he likes you a lot, Paddy. He told me you're his favourite little brother.'

'Yes, Mr Kidd, I like Brian a lot.'

'He's your favourite, isn't he, Paddy, just like you're his?'

'Yes, Mr Kidd, he's my favourite.'

'Good,' he said and stood up to go. I had no idea what that little chat with Mr Kidd meant or why he had asked me these questions and didn't think any more about it. Then he announced that we were going to the pictures with Miss Birkenhead to see *Summer Holiday*, starring Cliff Richard.

Soon after, we were told that we would be moving to a children's home. Brian and me were to be sent to a place called Westfield, and Michael, Claudette and my foster brother Ben were going to Parkfield. We were going to be separated for the very first time in our lives.

10

The first thing I noticed on our way to Westfield was that it was very close to Sefton Park, one of my old haunts when I was sagging school, so I knew then that we were not all that far from 'the Eight'. As we turned into Greenbank Drive it suddenly became dark, but that had nothing to do with the weather; in fact, it was a nice bright sunny afternoon. It was the trees and the hedges that were making the place seem overcast. But once we had set foot inside the home on the other side it was like walking into a botanical garden. Flowerbeds in the pattern of the Union Jack, apple and pear trees were dotted all around, and bordering the whole garden were strawberry plants and blackberry bushes. The whole place had a light, airy feeling about it and when the sun was shining on the garden it was beautiful.

We were welcomed by a woman called Mrs Greenall who signed us in and then took us upstairs where we were each kitted out with new play clothes and shoes and sandals, as well as new Sunday suits which resembled the old demob issue. Then we were taken to our dormitories, which all looked out on to the lawn; each room contained five or six beds. By now a lot of the other children had returned from school and had changed into their play clothes, and were now ready to sit down and have their tea. The dining room was quite large and held at least seven tables, with eight kids at each one, and on some (but not all) of the tables a member of staff would sit at the head.

After our first meal we were then given assignments to do: they were to be our duties as soon as we returned home from school each day. My duty was to polish all the shoes for school the next morning, and our Brian's job was to help out in the boiler room, keeping the central heating going and making sure there was enough hot water.

One of the boys there was a rebel, but a likeable one. His name was Alex and he and his mum had lived opposite Auntie Pat's flat in Upper Canning Street, but on the landing below us. He was mates with my brother Paul, but I was too young at the time and didn't remember him from those days. We became friends almost from the first day when Brian and me joined all the other boys on the playing field and I brought him down playing football. I was playing in defence when Alex came hurtling towards me at such speed that I just stuck my foot out and closed my eyes, hoping to get a tackle in. Alex saw this and just danced around me. I did catch him on the shin and bring him down but he still managed to keep hold of the ball, get up and score a fantastic goal. On the way back to his own half he patted me on the back and with a wry smile on his face, said 'Nice tackle, Ned', referring to the donkey kick of a tackle I had just made. And from then on the name stuck. Before the week was up everyone was calling me Ned

— all the kids, even Mr and Mrs Greenall and the rest of the staff, unless of course I was in trouble. Then it was 'Go and tell Paddy Barber I want to see him.'

Alex was a big Beatles fan and so were all the girls in the home. We sang along to all their hits and to those of other groups such as the Swinging Blue Jeans, Billy J. Kramer and the Dakotas and even the Searchers. The lead singer of the Searchers, Mike Curtis, had a distinct way of holding his guitar when they were singing 'Needles and Pins' (it always came out as 'Needles and Pinzzaah'), and I used to make Alex laugh when I did my impression of him. He always encouraged me to do more impersonations of other singers. We particularly liked the soul groups at the time although there was only one that I was familiar with. They just happened to be from Liverpool, and the first time we saw them on the telly was on a show called *Thank Your Lucky Stars*. The group was called the Chants.

Alex was always talking about the Beatles, how John Lennon was his idol and how he wanted to be like him. Well, I looked up to Alex and wanted to be like him so I too became a John Lennon fan. All the girls in the home adored Paul and George purely because of their babyish good looks, but people loved Lennon because he was the most outspoken and he wasn't afraid of letting people know that he came from Liverpool. Alex was like that, too, and that's what endeared me to him, what made me look up to him. He was a fantastic football player; he made me stand up to the ball when it came at me full force from a powerful left foot or a header and he was a joy to watch on the pitch, like George Best would be in years to come, and he was a lot of fun to be with.

All the kids seemed to get on with each other very well. On Saturday mornings we used to get our pocket money, put on our donkey jackets (these were tough jackets most commonly worn by labourers on building sites) and go down to the café in the park. We'd spend most of the mornings there drinking cups of Oxo and wandering about the park looking for birds' nests, eventually finding ourselves in Lark Lane, at the other side of the park, in another café drinking yet more cups of Oxo.

Once I was looking for nests with one of my old friends from the convent who was now at Westfield too. His name was Peter and in the convent he was known as 'Cobbler'. We came across this old boathouse in the park, and we could see up into the eaves and bits of nest sticking out. We decided to go and get them, but it meant crossing the moat which surrounded it. Peter had begun to climb the small bridge when a policeman came along, walking his pushbike, and asked me what I was doing hanging around the boathouse. I told him I was waiting for a friend; but he knew where Peter was and told him to come out from behind the boathouse. He could tell we were from Westfield by our donkey jackets but said he wasn't going to report us. He just told us to be careful and to stay out of any trouble, then slowly went on about his business.

Peter and I looked at each other and gave a sigh of relief.

'Cor, that was close, Cobbler,' I said to him.

That immediately upset him.

'Never call me that again,' he said.

'Why?' I asked. 'That's what we always called you in the convent.'

'I hated that name and I don't want to be reminded of it,' he snapped. He then told me that he hadn't been given the name because he had to clean and polish all the shoes but because he used to wear the soles of his shoes out very quickly. The nuns would make him wear working men's boots instead of ordinary shoes like the rest of us. They would also put loads of studs in the soles, making them very heavy and uncomfortable. I remembered how we were humiliated when we wet the bed. We were all kids being punished for something we couldn't help. I had a sudden flashback.

★   ★   ★

It was a Sunday morning and I had been through the usual ritual of cleaning up after wetting the bed and had then gone to my locker to get out my Sunday suit. When I opened the locker instead of my suit there was a girl's dress on the hanger. I stood there not quite knowing what to do when a voice behind me said, 'What's the matter?' I turned to see one of the female members of staff standing behind me with her arms folded and a cruel grin on her face.

'I don't know, Miss,' I replied. 'My suit doesn't seem to be here.'

'Well, where is it?' she asked.

'I don't know, Miss,' I said again.

Then she said, 'Well, what is there?'

'I don't know, Miss. There seems to be a girl's dress here.'

'Well,' she said, 'I suppose you had better put that on then, hadn't you?'

I looked at her, thinking, praying, that this was a joke. I couldn't speak. I half smiled at her as if to say, very funny, Miss, but she wasn't laughing. She took the dress from the hanger, undid the back and ordered me to put it on. Then she grinned, took me firmly by the hand and led me down the stairs, along the corridor and towards the chapel.

Opening the chapel door, she pushed me in. This woman was going to go through with this whole charade — she was relentless and unforgiving — and I thought, all this just for wetting the bed. She still had a firm grip on my hand as she made her way, with me in tow, towards the centre of the pews where the girls were. She made them all stand up so we could pass and she sat me down right in the middle of them. The tears were streaming down my face, just as they were now at the memory of the humiliation.

I felt a hand on my face and the feel of Peter's thumb wiping away a tear. 'Come on, mate, let's go and get a cup of Oxo down the café.'

'Why do people want to do those things to others, Peter?' I asked.

'Because they're shite,' he said, and we walked on, arms on each other's shoulders.

★ ★ ★

Peter's job in Westfield was to look after the boilers and oven maintenance in the kitchen, a job I was soon to end up doing till the time I left. Peter showed me how everything worked in the boiler room, how to keep it going and maintain a certain pressure, how to remove clinkers and stoke the fire, etc. And it was the only place where we could get away from nosey kids and staff as they rarely made visits to the boiler room, and in a way it turned out to be our sanctuary, a place where we could sit and chat and have a smoke!

During one conversation Peter reminded me of the day back in the convent when we were playing in the boys' playroom with our toys. When important visitors came to the convent they were shown all around the grounds, the dormitories, the kitchens, the chapel and finally the boys' and the girls' playroom. On this particular day the sister superior came in with a group of people. I noticed that one of the visitors was black. Who's this man, I thought to myself; is he my dad? He's black, I'm black, so he must be my dad. The sister pointed out various kids in the playroom to him and he went over to them and had little chats with each kid. Eventually he was introduced to me.

'And what's your name, young man?' he said as he shook my hand.

'Patrick,' I said. 'Patrick Barber,'
'And where are you from, Patrick?'
'Africa,' I said.

The man smiled and said, 'Africa? That's nice, Patrick, and what do you want to be when you grow up?'

'A fire engine,' I replied. Peter was standing nearby and started to laugh along with the man. I wasn't sure what they were laughing about, but when the man moved on to another boy Peter pulled me to one side and said, 'You don't come from Africa. You were born in Liverpool 8. You're a Scouse. You were born in Liverpool, England.'

'OK,' I said, 'but what's wrong with wanting to be a fire engine?'

★   ★   ★

In our time at Westfield we continued to attend our senior school, Cardinal Newman, but travelled to it by a new route, so we were all given bus passes.

Some of the kids had to attend a special school and I had been given the job of escorting one of the younger boys to his special bus which was on the way to my school. I had to take him to Penny Lane bus terminus where a bus would take him to school. His name was Jimmy, and he had two sisters, Eileen and Sally. Sally was the eldest of his family. Pretty soon it would be her turn to leave the care system and start out on her own. She was one of the favourites there and she was well liked by all the other kids and the staff, and when she left she was given a great send off.

A few weeks later, on a sunny autumn morning, I was walking little Jimmy to his bus stop down Greenbank Lane and through the park. As we turned into the park we could see a figure slumped over a park bench, looking lost and dishevelled. Just then a police car pulled up and two policemen got out and walked towards the bench. They had a blanket of some sort which they gently wrapped around the person. As we got closer we realised that it was Sally. Jimmy immediately started to cry and to shout over to his sister, but she couldn't hear him.

'What are they doing to my sister,' he cried. 'Where are they taking her? What has she done? She's not a criminal, leave her alone.'

All I could do was stand there and keep a firm hold of Jimmy's hand. His face was creased up in pain and confusion. Sally just wore a look of complete sadness, which said it all for me. Was this all there was when you came out of care? I turned Jimmy's head away and we walked slowly on.

Punishments were regularly meted out to the boys, such as the time when one of the elder boys tried to run away but was returned by the police. It was late at night and we were woken by shouting and loud thumps, which turned out to be the sound of fists landing squarely on the chest of this poor boy. If we had a grievance with each other, however, Mr Greenall would take us to the cellar or the garage and make us put on boxing gloves and thrash it out. This often meant that you were put in the ring against someone far smaller than you, some tiny tot who could come at you like a gnat. You'd just have to brush him away to a background of constant jibes from the other boys. Finally, you'd have to swat the poor kid so that he didn't come back for more. It wasn't pleasant but it was better than being on the receiving end of a grown-up's fist.

11

Our first summer holiday at Westfield was in North Wales, at a little holiday camp called St Mary's, in Gronant. Overlooking the camp site, high on a hill, was a small monastery called Talacre Abbey. The older boys would sleep in tents and the younger ones and the girls all slept in the chalets. Meals would be had in one of the chalets and the washing and baths in another. Brian was very popular with the girls and he loved dancing and was always eager to teach the girls the latest steps. Mr G's daughter Rita was a big pop fan — she always bought the latest records — and Mr G had his big Bush record player, with an amazing amplified extension speaker. You could say it was sort of a first stereo and he also used to love taking movies of all the kids enjoying themselves, dancing to the music, playing football, swimming and so on. And when we got back home he would put the music to the film and every once in a while we would watch it. Just as I wanted to be the loudest in the band when I was at St Sebastian's, so my acting here was really over the top, too. Some might say more or less how it is today!

During the day we played football and rounders and in the evenings we would be given our pocket money and driven into Rhyl, the mecca of North Wales, for a few hours. We were driven to the car park just round the back of the funfair, where we all piled out and split up into small groups of four or five. The girls tended to go with the girls and the boys — well, they just went. We tried everything — the ghost train, the big dipper, the bumper cars, and went into every arcade.

There were lots of smiles over that summer holiday, but sadness loomed over me as it came to the end because my two best friends, Alex and Peter, and my brother Brian were leaving. They were going to another home, one for young working boys.

They had just left school and were about to make their way into the big world. Brian left school a kind of folk hero in my eyes, and in the eyes of the majority of school kids as well, because of the way he stood up to this lad called Graham who thought he was smarter than the rest of us. One day he decided to tell all my classmates that I was a bed-wetter, even though Brian had warned him against doing so. He taunted me all the way to school. Brian was walking slightly ahead, humming a Cliff Richard song called 'Don't Talk to Him', so Graham started on him. Brian carried on humming until Graham was actually shouting in his ear. Suddenly Brian's fist landed squarely on Graham's jaw. He dropped to the ground like a stone and remained there until the ambulance men stretchered him into the back of the ambulance. The headmaster told us that the Barber family would come to nothing and that he would be informing the children's home. That's as may be, but no one had ever seen an actual live knockout punch and it was the talk of the school.

It was only at school that I got to see our Michael and Ben. I hardly saw Claudette at all as she was at a girls' school. They seemed to be having a nicer time at Parkfield and were allowed to call their staff auntie and uncle. It sounded more homely and I was a bit envious of them, but at the same time I was happy for them. I remember asking our new welfare officer, Mr Andrews, why we'd been split up and why we couldn't all be together. He replied, 'Well, you said you wanted to be with your older brother.'

'Yes,' I said, 'but I didn't say I didn't want to be with my other brothers and sister.' I then realised that thanks to Mr Kidd's clever questioning I had been the one to decide who went with whom.

I said to Mr Andrews, 'How long have we got to stay here?' He said, 'Only till we can find you a place where you can all be together again', and for the remainder of my time there I clung on to his last words: 'Only till we can find you a place where you can all be together again.'

I was a keen swimmer and at every opportunity to do extra swimming I was there. I wanted — and tried desperately — to get into the school swimming team but Mr Brennan, the gym teacher, sometimes refused even to acknowledge that I was there. Like the time of the annual swimming gala held at Queen's Drive baths. Our best swimmer was, of course, chosen to represent the school. When he didn't turn up, I approached Mr Brennan and told him that I was prepared to step in. He completely ignored me and walked away, leaving me standing there at the side of the pool. As an eager boy clutching his trunks and towel, I was completely confused by his behaviour.

I couldn't understand why Mr Brennan wouldn't let me swim for the school or why he didn't select me for the school football team. I felt I was a good swimmer and, with an extra bit of football practice, I might have been good enough to play for the school. I was keen and wanted to represent my school so much. I turned up for every swimming and football practice but was always sent home before they even started. I remember once I was just standing there removing fluff from my belly button when he hit me over the back of the head. So I was somewhat taken aback years later when I was doing a series of *Only Fools and Horses* and Ben, who was by then an Assistant Director in social services, told me he had come across Mr Brennan, who approached him with a script he had written. He explained to Ben that when he was a sports teacher at the school he had been young, overenthusiastic and full of himself and that now he realised he might have been unfair towards some of the kids. He asked Ben if he would pass his script on to me to have a look and perhaps give my opinion. I completely ignored him and his request. Not out of spite; I just didn't want to have anything to do with him again.

Sometimes Mr Greenall, along with another male member of the staff, would take us on weekend camping trips. Once he took us to an old charabanc graveyard, with the idea of converting one of them into a mobile home for the next holiday; it was going to take a year to do that. So just before Christmas it was purchased and all through the rest of the winter we worked on converting the old bus. We took out some of the seats and turned them round to face each other, then we made tables to go between them and boards that could be fitted to rest between the seats, so turning them into beds. At the front of the bus we installed a full-size gas cooker which was going to be fed by two large Calor gas bottles. Then a large wooden container had to be fitted on top of the bus. The bus had to be sent to a metal workers' yard to have a giant roof rack frame welded on to it, in order to hold this enormous box on top. It was ready in just under six months, six months ahead of schedule.

That Christmas we were all getting into the festive spirit. Preparing for it was exciting, putting up the Christmas tree and decking the hallway with brightly coloured lights. Mr Greenall had asked us a few weeks before what our first-choice present would be. I don't remember asking for anything specific but I got a bicycle. There was one condition, however; the bike had to remain at the home when it was time for me to leave. It was an old butcher's bike, which had had the basket frame removed. I rode to school on it every day right up to the time that I left. I also had to use it to run errands for Mr Greenall. Every time he ran out of cigarettes he would wake me up, sometimes late at night, to cycle to the all-night garage to get them for him.

Our Claudy. Taken in 1961

Our Brian. Taken in 1966 when he joined the army

Me, Claudy, Brian and Mike. Still smiling after all these years

Westfield Children's Home. Taken on a visit to Liverpool many years later

A night out with the girls after work when I was living at Sydney House

Alvin, Ben and me when we had just formed our group Soul Motion

The boy band grows up!

My first professional performance in 1970, playing Hud in *Hair*

Liverpool Daily Post & Echo

Hands up, those who want to get their kit off! There was a nude scene in *Hair* and I was one of the performers who didn't mind stripping off in front of a live audience. Early preparation for *The Full Monty*!

Liverpool Daily Post & Echo

Playing the role
of Caiaphas, the
high priest, in
*Jesus Christ
Superstar*

*Ronald Grant
Archive*

In another scene we were just about to crack up laughing
at someone's wisecrack. On the far left is my good friend
Larrington Walker

Liverpool Daily Post & Echo

My television debut in a 'Play for Today' called *Lucky*. We
were filming in Sefton Park in Liverpool. My mum used to
bring me here when I was a kid

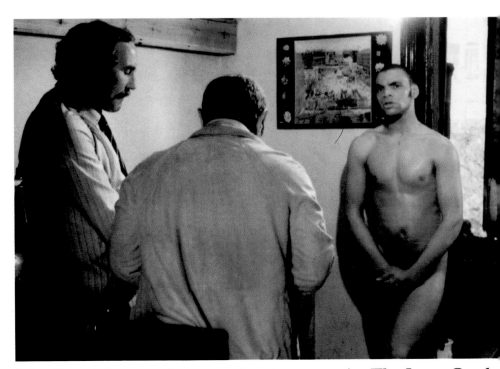

My film debut, and one and only scene, in *The Long Good
Friday*. I played Errol the Ponce

Me with some fellow actors from the television series *Gangsters*. I played Pick Axe Pete

BBC Photo Library

In a scene from *Gangsters* where we were preparing for a gang fight   *BBC Photo Library*

With Alan Igbon in *The Front Line*. We first met when I was performing in *Hair*. Alan was in the audience and I invited him up on stage

BBC Photo Library

With Phil Whitchurch in *The Brothers McGregor*. We played
half-brothers who ran a dodgy car dealership
BBC Photo Library

With Robbie Carlyle and Linus Roache on location in
Liverpool for the film *Priest*

Ronald Grant Archive

Playing Denzil in *Only Fools and Horses*. This is taken from the 'Heroes and Villains' episode with the famous Batman and Robin scene   *BBC Photo Library*

This is from 'To Hull and Back', which was my first Christmas special, and when I was asked by John Sullivan and Ray Butt if I'd like to be one of the gang

BBC Photo Library

Peckham's Finest!

BBC Photo Library

The Magnificent Seven! This was taken moments after we had shot the final scene of *The Full Monty*

I still don't know what the Arsenal offside trap is!

Ronald Grant Archive

I had a frozen shoulder when I shot this scene so I was a bit slow doing the full monty!

At the premiere of Samuel L. Jackson's film *Eve's Bayou*. Later we worked together in the film *The 51st State*

Wenn/Michael Williams

Filming *The Virgin of Liverpool* with Jake Abraham, Ricky Tomlinson and Ian Puleston-Davies

Liverpool Daily Post & Echo

Playing the part of Paul, a hard nightclub bouncer in *Dead Man's Cards*. Same name but very different role for me

Liverpool Daily Post & Echo

In a scene with the late Tom Bell and James McMartin who wrote the film

Liverpool Daily Post & Echo

An actor's life can be tough sometimes, but someone's got to do it!

Empics

Some Christmas present. I remained at Westfield for at least another two years and during that time I was to have two more summer holidays with them, the last one on the converted bus. We toured all the Welsh seaside towns, driving down to Aberystwyth and then much further afield, to Exeter and Dawlish.

I remember a whole lot of us going to a fair in Dawlish once. As usual we went in small groups so as not to look too prattish. Our group came face to face with a bunch of yobs who started on the usual, name calling and taunting. They didn't know that this time Mr G was with us, but a little behind the group. When we caught up with them they'd got back to their parents or guardians and we were about to lay into them. One of the parents threatened to call the police, at which point Mr G turned up. We told him what had happened and he came good for us. These lads, he said, spend 365 days a year cramped up in a children's home, without their real parents. Some of them come from broken homes and some of them are difficult to handle. If your boys don't apologise you may have to call the police to help me drag my boys off the heads of yours . . . They came to their senses.

Not long after the holidays were over I was told that I would be joining my brothers Brian and Michael with new foster parents somewhere in Anfield. I felt a little bit sad because, once again, I was going to have to say ta-ra to all my friends at the home. By now I had become one of the favourites there, although I wasn't getting my own way or anything like that. It was just this kind of mutual respect that I was given by the kids and the staff. There was no mention of my sister Claudette joining us, and I wasn't too happy about that, but at least I would be with my brothers. On the day I left all the kids and staff came to the gates to wave goodbye and see me off. Sad though I was to be leaving all my friends behind, I could now look forward to a new life with my new foster parents. And anyway, I didn't really think it was going to be the last time I saw them. I knew that some of us would probably meet up in another home somewhere along the way.

12

On the way to my new foster home I remembered when Mrs Allen had first come to visit me with her son Jim and the welfare officer. I didn't have much to say but I was afraid to ask any questions. I wasn't quite sure if I really wanted to go. It wasn't the upheaval of leaving Westfield — I was used to moving from place to place — but I still had vivid memories of how unhappy life had been at Mary's. At least, I thought, I'll be with Brian and Michael. But that reunion was short-lived.

Mrs Allen was a widow and as well as her son Jim she had two daughters. Brian was working now and Michael and I were still at school. I knew in the first couple of weeks that I wasn't going to be happy there, especially as, soon after I arrived, Michael had to leave. Not long after that Brian left too.

One day Mrs Allen and Sandy, one of the girls, were in the back room leading to the kitchen, and Mike was upset about something. She asked him in front of her daughter what was wrong. I knew he was going to have trouble getting his words out and I also knew the matter was trivial and that I could easily answer it for him. I hated seeing him being made to struggle to get his words out and getting more stressed and anxious about it. I told Michael not to bother answering and was told to shut up. They carried on taunting him and laughing at him. When he finally got his words out, they made him say it again, under the pretext that they hadn't quite heard him. I was so mad and angry at them I cried with rage, but not in front of them. I wasn't going to give them the chance to say, 'Cry more, pee less', as they often did to Mike and me.

Jim was the only member of the family who treated us with affection and I got on well with him. Life was bearable when he was around. When he wasn't I would go upstairs and play my records as I couldn't bear to be in the same room with just Sandy and Mrs A. Whereas Sandy was always moody, Jim was always having a laugh and loved to play jokes on everyone. He had a job as a plasterer and came home every night with his plastering board and trowel sticking out of his army-type rucksack. His overalls were always covered in plaster and splashes of paint. When Jim was in a playful mood, which was more often than not, he would grab hold of me, put me in a head lock, ruffle my hair and wrestle me to the ground, tickling me until I screamed, 'I give in, I give in', and if he hadn't shaved for a few days then he would grab my head in both hands and rub his rough stubble, which felt like coarse sand-paper, all over my cheeks. He was the life and soul of a house which didn't seem to me to have much of either. He was about twenty and had a special relationship with Lassie, the dog. She'd hear Jim coming home from work, whistling at the top of the road, and her ears would go up into a state of alertness. Jim would be all over Lassie, ruffling her ears, patting her belly, winding her up into a fever pitch of excitement. Then he'd bound upstairs to get cleaned up and ready to go out with his mates, bound down again, have his tea, before dropping off for forty winks, with Lassie sprawled at his feet in front of the fire.

One day Jim was getting ready to go out. I'd noticed a dark blue Jaguar parked outside and he told me it was his new car. I thought how cool it would be to be seen getting out of that outside my school. So I was chuffed when he said he would take me to school one morning. I told him I wanted to see him behind the wheel and asked him if he was going out it in that night. He said, 'No, not tonight, because I'm going to be drinking and it's not good to drink and drive.'

In the early hours of the morning we were woken up by a policeman who told Mrs A that Jim had been involved in a road accident on the East Lancs Road. He had to have his arm amputated and when he eventually returned home he was a changed man. He was able to walk and get around but every now and again he would just break down in tears, sobbing uncontrollably. The happy-go-lucky Jim was gone and we were both sad. Sometimes he would try to cheer me up by rubbing his bandaged stump on my cheeks, which I didn't think was funny, but I would put on a brave face and smile. I never really knew what to say to Jim after the accident and I never ever asked him what exactly happened that night, but I would spend long hours just sitting with him as he nodded off in front of the fire, with Lassie the dog our only company. Now, years later, whenever I see 'don't drink and drive' campaign advertisements I think of Jim. He couldn't drive and of course he didn't own the Jag. He just said it to keep up the pretence. He didn't know that what he was saying was years ahead of its time.

Now that Mike and Brian had left, and with what had happened to Jim, I was feeling more and more isolated and more lonely. To this day I don't really know why Brian left and he could never remember exactly what caused him to do so. By this time anyway we'd all been moved from pillar to post so many times; welfare officers and social workers talked a lot *about* you to work colleagues but never *to* you, the person whose life they were deciding on. If you were being moved, as a child you were invariably the last to know about it. You went where they sent you. For me it was a bit like being in a plane crash: going in and out of a deep coma and coming round each time to find you were with a different family, among new faces. I didn't have any friends in that area so sometimes I would walk miles just to go and see my friends from St Sebastian's, Paul Giles and the Kelly twins.

My room now became a retreat and I would spend hours there just daydreaming, wondering if, like the places before, I would ever get out of there. Sometimes I would go into the front parlour and play Sandy's records on her Dansette record player, or listen to her transistor radio. Radio Caroline, one of the first pirate (i.e. unlicensed) radio stations, had just started up and music was by now my only means of comfort. I would get lost in the songs and the beats and rhythms, the Walker Brothers singing 'The Sun Ain't Gonna Shine Anymore', Len Barry's '1-2-3', the Rolling Stones and 'The Last Time', and Bob Dylan singing 'Subterranean Homesick Blues'. Even Barry McGuire's 'Eve of Destruction'. A lot of the songs were purely pop-orientated, but some, like 'Eve of Destruction', that were coming into the charts now had more meaning to them and I found myself listening to the words and really digesting them. They seemed to carry me onwards and some of them were even uplifting. Mrs A was forever having a go at me and she would always end her little tirades with the words, 'You want a job doing you might as well do it yourself. Get out of me road.'

On one such occasion she admonished me for something that hadn't gone right. In my frustration I stormed out of the kitchen yanking the handle off the door as I slammed it behind me, effectively locking Mrs A inside. So I opened the door again and gave the handle back to her. I think she had just been waiting for an excuse to get rid of me and it was only a matter of days before she called my welfare officer. So not only did I get out of her road but I got out of her house as well.

This time I was going to Parkfield. Ben and Mike had already been moved by the time I got there so I didn't know when we would be together again. I just had to make do with seeing them at school. I hadn't heard much about

Claudy except that she had been moved to a young girl's working hostel. I was looking forward to going to Parkfield as it had seemed so much nicer than Westfield. Kids seemed to have much more freedom around the house.

13

It was March 1966, the year of the World Cup in England, when I arrived at Parkfield. It looked small from the outside, but inside it was spacious. I was greeted at the door by a tall, quite wiry lady. She was called Auntie Viv and I went through the usual formalities of being signed in, taken to the wardrobe room and shown the dormitory. Things were run differently here from Westfield. Each home had its own set of house rules; some places were very strict with the rules and others were quite easy-going. Westfield was slightly tougher in the sense that if you did something really bad then you were suitably punished; at Parkfield if you did something really bad it seemed to go unnoticed, whereas if you did something trivial you were beaten for it. My first week there I was slippered by Auntie Viv and caned by Uncle George, once for the most trivial of things and the other time for something of which I was completely innocent. The first time I was in the playroom throwing a ball up against the wall, which, unbeknownst to me, was the other side of Auntie Viv's office. She walked into the playroom and ordered me to her office. She then produced a slipper from under her desk and laid into me. I was almost in tears. I hadn't expected it to hurt as much as it did because whenever we were punished by a female member of staff we didn't expect to be hit so hard. The second time I was punished was on my first Sunday there. I got up, washed and put on my Sunday suit. Those of us who were Catholic had to wait until we had come back from mass before we could have breakfast because we were going to receive Holy Communion. Those who were Church of England had breakfast first and then went off to church. When our service was over we returned to the home and settled down to our breakfast, by which time the other kids had returned.

Suddenly, from out of nowhere, a man I had never seen before walked into the dining room and ordered all the boys into his office. For some reason he looked like an American GI: wearing combat-like fatigues and sporting a crew cut. Straightaway I thought, this must be Uncle George; now is my chance to say hello. Well, when we walked into the office he turned on us and said, 'I have had a report from the church that most of you boys have been misbehaving, and I'm going to make sure you don't do it again.' Then, from behind the desk, he produced a thinnish but swishy cane and told the first boy to bend over. He gave him six of the hardest, leaving him in tears. All the other boys awaited their punishment in silence. It was only then that I noticed that the boys in the room hadn't been in the same church as me. I raised my hand to attract Uncle George's attention and to point out that I really didn't think I should be there. He half looked at me while he was thrashing away at the next boy and said to me, 'Don't try and worm your way out of this, sonny. It just makes

96

me more angry. You will take your punishment like a man.'

My buts and protestations fell on deaf ears. It was my turn now and reluctantly I bent over the desk and six thwacks of the cane descended on my buttocks. I returned tear-stained to the kitchen. I'd been mistaken for a Proddy and caned for it.

My time in Parkfield was short, perhaps even shorter than our stay in New Heys, and the only thing that was carrying me through these places was the music. The Beatles had been around for a bit but now everybody was talking about them all over the country. They were local boys, of course, making good, popular music and bringing out hits one after another as if on a production line. Our Michael was always humming 'Eight Days a Week' and we kids were always discussing our favourite songs. I knew almost every lyric the Beatles wrote. It became almost a mark of disloyalty not to sing along to one of their songs. There was a feeling of pride that you were born in the same city as the Beatles.

There was, too, always one kid in your class whose dad had gone to the same school as John Lennon, or whose auntie lived next door to Ringo's mum. You would listen open-mouthed as they claimed, 'My auntie's best friend lives two doors away from Paul McCartney's sister', or 'George's mum goes into my uncle's shop every day to get her shopping!'

14

One day while I was playing in the schoolyard a kid from the year below came up to me. His name was Mike Carney. He had been in the first year when Brian had knocked out that boy Graham and said he would never forget it for the rest of his life. Then he got on to the subject of homes and asked what it was like being in care. I told him that each child in care had a welfare officer whose job it was to try and find foster parents to take us in and bring us up as one of the family. He asked me if I had a welfare officer. I told him I had, that his name was Mr Andrews and that he drove a red and cream Comer van. Mike said he had seen him visiting a house opposite where he lived in Garston. I then told him there was a strong possibility that I might be going there as there was some talk back at the home that my stay at Parkfield was nearing its end. Mike got really excited at the thought and as my day of departure approached he kept me up to date with the comings and goings of Mr Andrews.

In May 1966 I finally moved from Parkfield. The moment Mr Andrews and I pulled up outside my new house, I looked across the road at the house opposite and there stood Mike, grinning and waving at me. I waved back, grinning too. Then I went inside and was introduced to my new family, Mr and Mrs Banks and their four children, three of whom — Sarah, Peter and Claire — were fostered and the youngest, Adam.

I now seemed further away from Liverpool 8 than ever before.

Claire was a very small, elflike and hypersensitive figure. You never wanted to be in the same room when she kicked off for what seemed like no apparent reason. She reminds me, in hindsight, of a younger version of Sissy Spacek in *Carrie*. If you talked to her or raised your voice slightly to her she would just scream hysterically. There was never any point in telling her to calm down or anything like that; you just left the room and let her get on with it. Peter was a very quiet kid who sometimes looked a bit wide-eyed, vacant; you were never sure if he was going to speak to you or ask you a question. He just stared at you. Then there was Sarah who was a year or two older than me and she was a real stunner. I was fifteen and just becoming sexually aware and I was very attracted to her. I hadn't thought about sex before now and never discussed it with my mates at school, but every time I saw Sarah or was close to her I could feel these sexual stirrings, which confused me even more because she was supposed to be my sister.

I was also coming up to my last year in school, and I wasn't quite sure how I was going to deal with leaving school and starting work. In the months leading up to it, Mr Andrews took me to careers centres to look for suitable jobs and there was also the possibility of joining Mr Banks at the Dunlop factory just up the road at Speke.

But as I and my friends in care were in the lower stream at school there was little chance of any of us getting a good, well-paid job. At fifteen, the future looked a bit bleak for me. But throughout my childhood, from the moment I entered the care system, it was not overall an easy ride. Whereas some of my other schoolfriends had parents who were working and who could perhaps help put them in the right direction after they left school, I never really had anyone who was interested in my future.

When I wasn't thinking about Sarah or looking for a job I spent my time listening to Radio Caroline, which had now been on the air for two years. Apart from the Beatles and the Rolling Stones, the music of the Kinks (' Sunny Afternoon'), Chris Farlowe ('Out of Time'), Lulu, Ike and Tina Turner ('River Deep, Mountain High'), Lorraine Ellison ('Stay With Me Baby'), Donovan, the Small Faces, the Monkees ('I'm a Believer'), the Lovin' Spoonful ('Daydream'), Dave Dee, Dozy, Beaky, Mick & Titch, the Tremeloes, Dave Davies, The Move ('Flowers in the Rain') Flowerpot Men ('Let's Go to San Francisco') and the Young Rascals ('Groovin'') all filled my head. I would spend hours in the garden just listening to those beautiful songs. Music was never better.

Mr Andrews eventually got me a job in a small factory, a plastics firm which specialised in making scent-bottle tops, just around the corner from Parkfield. My job was to remove these plastic scent-bottle tops from the rotating machine and then place a small rounded piece of cardboard on the inside. This was called wadding. It was one of the most boring and monotonous jobs anyone could wish upon a fifteen-year-old. I lasted three weeks.

Coming home with my third and final wage packet did not go down well with Mrs Banks and the next day my lunchbox was empty. She made it clear that I was not to hang about the house but to find another job immediately. I got one in a bottle-cleaning factory called King's of Garston. The empties, mainly Guinness bottles, would arrive at one end of the factory, be loaded on to the washing machine and arrive at the other end of the conveyor belt cleaned and relabelled, ready to be filled with Guinness again.

I rode my bike to work but was getting punctures almost every day because of the broken glass everywhere. Well, that job didn't last long either and the looks from Mrs Banks weren't getting any friendlier, so I was off again, hitting the road to seek employment elsewhere. I was beginning to get the hang of this short-term employment lark; I even had the gall to go back to the very first factory I'd worked in. They took me on and gave me the very same job. Every so often the foreman would look at me and say, 'You know what, I'm sure I've seen you before but I just can't think where.' And off he would go, scratching his bonce. The deception didn't last, though, and before long I was given my cards and told to leave. A week or so later I had started work at Grahams Cartons and my lunchbox was filled once more.

I still couldn't stop thinking about Sarah and I could make almost any song fit one of the many images of her in my head. My emotions were at complete loggerheads with the fact that she was my foster sister and it wasn't *right* to feel this way about her. Or was it? I didn't have anybody to talk to about this confusion and I grew more and more frustrated.

One day at work my bike was written off by a van. I was gutted and almost in tears. I was saving up for the holidays and was hoping to cycle to North Wales. Ernie, my boss, could see how upset I was and said, 'Pat, look, I've got a bike at home. It's a racing bike and it's got five speeds and Benelux gears. You can have it for a fiver if you work one late night. Deal?'

That night I went to bed imagining myself on the road to Prestatyn.

I spent the next few weeks in training, so to speak, for the big journey by cycling to Formby and other places in and around Liverpool. When the day came to leave, the rest of the family packed the suitcases and themselves into the Morris Traveller. I was given directions on how to get to the holiday camp, even though I knew the way from other trips.

I started out an hour before the rest of the family and made my way to the Pier Head. I got a real sense of freedom the moment I disembarked from the Mersey ferry. I was on my own and there was nobody around to tell me what to do. The road was mine and I was going to enjoy every moment of it. As I cycled along I thought about Brian, Mike and Claudy. I went past the very first camp site I'd been to when I was in Westfield and it brought back memories of happier times: pitching the tents, the army camp beds, the charabanc that we transformed for the holiday, the trips into Rhyl, the funfair, the girls and Brian dancing round the record player, Mr Greenall filming it all on his cine-camera.

By the time the Morris Traveller passed me, the horn honking as it did so, I was halfway to Palins Holiday Camp and reached it just as they were unloading. For the first time I knew the true meaning of saddlesore, but nevertheless it was a great ride. I hardly used the bike for the first few days I was there, but once the pain had subsided in my bum cheeks I was back in the saddle and I was able to get away into the hills.

The holidays got off to a good start, and there was plenty to do in the arcades, but sometimes I hung around the camp. One day I wandered over to the bingo hall where I could hear music. It was empty except for a lone figure stacking up the shelves with prizes.

'Come on in, son. If you've got nothing to do, do you want to give me a hand?' He seemed friendly so I said yes. His name was Ben and I went back the next couple of days, enjoying helping out and listening to the music. Being into the Beatles and the Stones and just about everyone else who was in the charts, I quite surprised myself when I went to put Nat 'King' Cole on the record player. I found I liked his sound and songs like 'There Was A Boy', 'Delilah', 'The Little Boy That Santa Claus

103

Forgot', 'Funny', 'Never Say Never' and many more.

I would go with Ben into Rhyl to get more supplies from the warehouse. We'd fill the car up with thermos flasks, cuddly toys, dinner sets, box spanner sets, pocket radios, furry steering wheel covers, car blankets and quilts and bring them back and set up for the next session.

One day Ben asked me to call out the numbers and he showed me how to use the machine. I was fascinated by the way it blew all the balls about in the glass case with only one ball making its way to the top of the plastic tube. I was a bit nervous at first but I soon got into my stride. 'Eyes down look in', 'Any line across, down, or from side to side, corner to corner and we're off', 'On the blue on its own number eight', 'Red, legs eleven', 'On the blue two fat ladies eighty-eight', 'On the yellow two and one twenty-one'. I grew more confident with each session and the holidaymakers didn't seem to notice my inexperience.

Sarah and I got on really well and most of the time we were hardly out of each other's company, but I never let on to her about the way I felt — even if I had wanted to, my lack of confidence would have prevented me.

At the start of the second week we met a young newly wed couple from Manchester called Mick and Sue, who took an immediate liking to Sarah and me. Mick was into music too and introduced me to the more meaningful sounds of Bob Dylan — 'Subterranean Homesick Blues', 'Like a Rolling Stone', 'Freewheelin'' and 'I

Want You'. At the end of the holiday we exchanged addresses and we were invited to go and stay with them in Manchester.

Mrs Banks wouldn't let us go together for some reason so we both had weekends by ourselves. It was my very first visit to Manchester. Mick and Sue met me at the station, and we drove back to their flat which was in a high-rise tower block. It took me a while to nod off that first night because I just kept thinking I was going to fall out of the window, even though my bed was on the opposite side of the room. I had a great time and visited a couple more times before Mrs Banks refused to let me go again. I was never sure why she did this. Perhaps she felt she had a responsibility to the welfare authorities and that we would need their permission to go to Manchester. That was the end of me going to see Mick and Sue.

As I was never allowed to use the bath at Mrs Banks's, every Saturday morning I'd make my way to Garston public baths and wait in the queue until there was a bath free. The baths were big and deep and had big brass taps on them but the taps didn't have any handle. If you wanted more hot water you had to ring this bell or pull on the cord and one of the bath attendants would come along with a key attached to a piece of string. She would come into your cubicle and top up the bath. It somehow never bothered me about women seeing me naked in the bath; we had staff in the homes seeing us almost every day with no clothes on at bathtime.

As with so much of what went on while I was

being fostered, it never occurred to me to question why Mrs Banks didn't want me using the bath at the house. Perhaps it was because I was beyond caring at that stage: three sets of foster parents and grief in all of them. No foster home I had been in ever truly made me feel part of the family so I suppose I just saw this as another way of excluding me. I wasn't sure I wanted to belong anyway. The trips to the market to get me second-hand clothes didn't make me feel special in any way; nor did the daily lunchbox with its tin of sardines, or the porridge every morning which was made the night before and warmed up again at breakfast time. But I quite liked going to the baths: I could take as long as I liked and was never rushed or told to hurry up.

After my bath I would change into my clean clothes and then go out for the afternoon or the remainder of the day. Sometimes when I was out of work I would walk miles to find employment. It was frustrating. I went to lots of big food factories, among them those making Jacob's Cream Crackers, Hartley's Jam, and the Tate & Lyle sugar and Crawford's biscuit factories (some of them probably swallowed up by a big conglomerate long ago), but I was never given a satisfactory answer as to why these big companies couldn't — or wouldn't — employ me. I was beginning to feel aware for the first time that my colour might have something to do with it.

Quite often I would go back to the children's home I had stayed in. I would get depressed when I looked at the kids through the windows, remembering what it had been like when I was there. There we were all treated more or less the same, not like in the foster homes where it was made perfectly clear that you were different. At least you'd felt reasonably safe in the homes. I used to think wistfully that maybe they would take me in, even though all the the kids I knew had long gone. The faces peering out at me now called 'Hey, Miss' to the window and I could see that it was a different miss from the one I'd known. I was fifteen and I felt so alone and ached to belong somewhere.

By now, my relationship with the family was beginning to deteriorate, as was the situation with Sarah. This was going to be my 'Paint It Black' period. My sexual attraction towards her was becoming stronger and therefore more difficult to cope with. It became a daily battle to fight my urges, which I didn't really understand. It reached a point when it was difficult being in the same room as her and I started finding myself criticising the way she dressed and responding sarcastically when she tried to make conversation with me. I know I was just trying to be cruel because she was the cause of my turmoil. I fancied her so much. On occasions I found myself sneaking into her room when no one was around. I would go through her cupboards and drawers, touching all her clothes and find myself getting aroused. I suppose it was only a matter of time before I got caught out.

One day I was sitting in the front room playing some new records I had just bought when Mrs

Banks popped her head around the door and said she was off to the shops and that she wouldn't be too long. As soon as she had gone I went upstairs to Sarah's room, opened her underwear drawer and pulled out a sort of camisole garment and held it next to my body. Suddenly I became aware of another presence in the room. I turned around and there in the doorway stood Mrs Banks. Her look of disgust froze me to the spot. 'Get downstairs at once,' she said slowly, deliberately and coldly, and turned on her heel. I wanted to plead with her to talk to me and help me, but I knew she had already built up a wall of silence. I felt as if iced water had been poured all over me and the pain and shame felt worse than any beating I had ever taken.

When I went downstairs and into the front room Mrs Banks was just putting the phone down. I knew she had been talking to my welfare officer. I walked over to a chair, sat down and lowered my head into my hands. My eyes welled up and the tears began to roll down my cheeks. I kept asking myself over and over again why this was happening to me. The image of little Jimmy Brady's sister being removed from a park bench came to mind. Was life just a dead end for kids who come out of care? Mrs Banks left the room. When the welly turned up it wasn't Mr Andrews but a big, burly man who looked more like a parole officer. Mrs Banks started to explain what she had found me doing while I sat there in silence. Bizarre as it may seem, I started thinking about how Radio Caroline had just been taken off the air because of some government legislation against pirate radio stations. I had listened to the final broadcast by the DJ Tony Prince and heard his heartfelt plea to the millions of faithful listeners who had tuned in to 199 Radio Caroline North, urging us all to keep free radio free and to keep the faith. I was crying when he came to the end of his speech and the airwaves fell silent. It was just loss upon loss.

The next morning the familiar green Liverpool Education minibus arrived at the house to pick me up and move me on. There was no looking back this time as I walked towards the bus. Sarah and Mrs Banks stood in the doorway. Sarah wasn't aware why I suddenly had to leave. I wanted to look back and say sorry to her, but all I could do was walk away without a word to either of them. The feelings of guilt and shame from that incident stayed with me for some years after, though I now know that what I was experiencing was normal for a boy of my age. The fact that the object of my attraction was my foster sister was something that could easily have been explained. I hadn't grown up with Sarah in a sister/brother relationship. We were just a boy and girl living in the same family. But I had no one to tell me this back then when I was a confused fifteen-year-old.

15

I was taken on a silent fifteen-minute ride to Sydney House, a hostel for young working lads on Linnet Lane. It was run by Mr Aspinall, a very large man. Mr Aspinall and the trouble-shooter exchanged a few words and then a delivery-type chit was signed and he was off. I felt like I was entering an institution for young offenders.

Every time you went to a new home you would always be asked by one of the other kids why you had had to leave your last place, like it was always your fault and that you deserved to be in a place like this. I couldn't bring myself to explain; all the things that had happened to me while I was in care were building up in my head. There seemed to be no end to this end-of-summer nightmare I was going through. I still had my job at Grahams Cartons with Ernie, which was a blessing. All it meant was that I now took a different route to work every morning. And now here I was in a working hostel for young men and having to adjust to settling down in this now totally male-dominated institution. Memories of the convent and Mary's reinforced the way I was feeling about myself once again — unwanted, unloved, distrusted, ugly and dirty. My head was full of guilt and confusion and I felt as if I was losing my way; some nights after work I would make to turn left to go home, back to the Banks's and Sarah, when I should have turned right to go the other way, to Sydney House.

Sydney House stood in its own grounds on the other side of Sefton Park. The house was big, almost Gothic-looking, with a short driveway leading to the porch steps and two bells to the right of the door, one daytime and the other night-time. To the back of the house there was a large lawn which backed on to the rear of another hotel overlooking the park itself, just across the way from Westfield, where I had been a few years earlier. There were a lot of children's homes and nursing homes for the elderly scattered around the park, and now I was once again just around the corner from Parkfield. Although all the occupants of Sydney House were men, there was only one female member of staff and she was the cook. She was only there in the mornings and early evening; she'd give you your breakfast then she would be off for the rest of the day and return again late afternoon to prepare the evening meals.

One of the first things I had to get used to was the order of the day — first up, best dressed. I soon found out what that meant when I came home from work one evening and found that half my wardrobe was missing. When I complained to Mr A he just said, 'It's every man for himself in this place', and to get used to it. Needless to say, I did.

At the end of the week you just handed in your wages and you were given what was left after they had taken your keep and clothes money,

111

laundry, etc. I was in a world of grown-ups now and I wasn't quite sure if I was ready for it. I had settled in at Sydney House but before long I lost my job and I was finding it increasingly hard to find another one. While you were unemployed you weren't allowed to hang about the house. You were given two sandwiches wrapped in foil and sent out to look for a job; you were not allowed to return until 5.30, when the gainfully employed got back. If you were in work and had a day off then you could hang around the house or play music.

Nearly every place I applied for a job there were no vacancies. I did the rounds again of a lot of the big factories on the outskirts of the city and walked along the Dock Road. I walked all over Liverpool looking for work and applying for jobs, all with no luck, until I eventually found one in a stocking factory called Bear Brand, packing stockings into boxes. My job was to run a machine that made the boxes. For some unknown reason among the girls I was one of the most popular lads on the floor. Then it became clear why. At the end of each shift the girls' handbags would be searched for stray stockings by the foreman or the security guard on the main gate that everyone had to pass through in the morning when they first arrived. The boys never got searched. I would always be chatted up by the girls and persuaded to put a few pairs of stockings inside my jeans, with the promise of a snog on delivery of the items after work. The promised snog would never arrive — you merely got a little peck on the cheek before the girls ran

112

off home — but you didn't mind because a peck on the cheek was better than nothing at all. That job didn't last long either; I got another one, though, working in a steel-container factory making steel drums for cooking oil and the like.

The end of summer '68 saw me working in a very popular store in Bold Street in the town centre called King Kong's. It was a discount store specialising in domestic appliances. One of the girls there was called Jean. She was married and looked like Dusty Springfield. I had a crush on her and wanted her to adopt me. We shared an interest in music and she loved the Supremes. She would often invite me back to her place and sometimes she would cook me a meal. For some reason it felt like I was back in the homes again; she had a motherly way about her and I loved the attention she gave me. Her handwriting was perfect, too; the way she wrote out those price tags and labels to display over the items in the window always fascinated me.

Back at the hostel I had made friends with a few of the lads. One worked in a tailor's shop and his knowledge of fashion and style never ceased to amaze me. He would always come home with the latest cut or fashion. Another worked in a record shop so I was always up on the latest releases. The Mods and Rockers were with us now. Mods sported Ben Sherman shirts and suits with pleats in the back of the jacket which went all the way up to the collar. Every lad who wore one had that Steve Marriott look about him, and the music was changing too — the Small Faces, Traffic, the Beatles, the

Rolling Stones and Engelbert Humperdinck. Words becoming more meaningful, more important, songs about love and hate, fortune and fame, losing and winning, sadness and loss, emotional songs sometimes reflecting the way I felt. This was a time when I had to confront my generation.

One evening while returning home from the cinema with Robbie and Steve, we were discussing the movie we had just seen, *Our Man Flint* starring James Coburn. We passed a pub and standing in the doorway was this Mod with his long, black, gaberdine-type coat, buttoned up to the collar. I wasn't paying that much attention but as we passed he said, 'What the fuck are you looking at, you black bastard?' Well, being into non-violence and still in summer of love mode, I chose to ignore the remark and carried on talking. Suddenly Robbie stopped me, grabbed me by the arm and said, 'Paddy, are you going to take that from that little shite, are you?'

I thought, yeh, your right Robbie, and with that I turned to face him and replied, 'I'm sorry, they don't label shit any more.' The next minute he pounced on me and brought me to the ground, fists flying everywhere. The boot was going in, the lot; it was a right free for all between the two of us. As I was on the ground fighting for my pride and honour, I couldn't help being reminded of the time a few years earlier at Parkfield when my friend Ray got into a fight he felt he'd been forced into. He was looking up at us and crying and pleading to us, 'Is this what you all want? Is this making you happy, seeing me beat the shite out of him?' This is how I felt as I sat astride this guy punching away. I thought it would all be over in a minute, but then someone shouted for help and suddenly about seventeen Mods came charging out of the pub and started on my mates. Now I was up to my neck in my first street brawl. It would not have been a memorable fight without the famous Kirby kiss — a head butt. We tried to make a run for it, but no sooner had we got halfway up the road than a Post Office van suddenly appeared at the top, blocking our escape route, and from the back of the van emerged another load of Mods, hungry for a rumble. Also coming at us from the other end of the lane, behind us, were about half a dozen scooters adorned with mirrors and foghorns. Now we were trapped and our only way of escape was through one of the side streets. Running towards it I tripped and fell. I could hear one of the scooters getting closer and, looking over my shoulder, I could see it coming towards me. The wheels, one after the other, ran over my body as I tried to roll out of the way. I felt like a human ramp for a skateboarder, but luckily enough when I stood up I felt no pain whatsoever. I just brushed myself down and managed to make my escape back to the safety of the house. When I got back, Stevie and Robbie were already sitting there and Robbie asked, 'What took you so long?' We could all laugh about it but at the end of the day we had stood up to them and put up a good fight.

I started taking a different way to work the next morning in order to avoid the pub where it had all kicked off. That was until my foster brother Ben turned up at the hostel. 'What's all this I hear about you getting into street brawls?' was the first thing he said to me, Completely ignoring the fact that I was gaping at him open-mouthed, wondering what the hell he had been up to, why he was here and why his face was all smashed up. It had been a good few years now since I'd last seen him and to see him like this came as a sickening shock. How could someone inflict so much damage on another person? Especially Ben, who had always been able to handle himself and come out of a scrap unscathed.

'What happened to you?' was my immediate question.

'Never mind about me,' he replied. 'What went on last night?' I lowered my head in a sort of heroic but bashful way, trying to avoid his questioning gaze.

'I'm OK,' I said. 'It was nothing really.' I wanted to make light of it all. I didn't want to tell him that I had tried to avoid confrontation by walking away and that it had taken a white boy to remind me that I was a human being, and that no one had the right to insult me or make derogatory remarks about my colour.

I told him then that I was now taking a different route to work. The next evening Ben came by again and whispered into my ear, 'It's safe now for you to go to work your usual way,' winking at me as he let go of my arm. I was a bit puzzled and asked, 'How do you make that out?' to which he replied, 'Mind your own business.'

116

'Fine,' I said. 'Nice one.'

Then he disappeared again as mysteriously as he had arrived. From then on I kind of looked upon him as my guardian angel, someone who turned up out of the blue, put things right, then pissed off again without so much as a by your leave. A short while after Ben left, Ray Lake and Paddy Nolan, two of the other lads who had been with me at Westfield, turned up at the hostel along with two new members of staff, Mr Culshaw and Mr Mitchell, both ex-army chappies. Mr Mitchell, who wore a kilt, was quiet and reserved. You didn't want to upset him or get in his way. He could handle himself as he was also an unarmed combat instructor, and most weekday evenings out on the back lawn he would give lessons in self-defence or, as he put it, unarmed combat. I attended most sessions. Even though it was a young man's working hostel, we were still governed by the house rules. The main rules in this place were no alcohol and no young women on or about the premises. So it was kind of embarrassing going for a drink with your mates and not being able to stand them a round, let alone get yourself one.

Soon it would be time for me to leave Sydney House and the care system, and this time it would be final. There would be no coming back for three meals a day, no clean clothes at the end of your bed, no clean sheets twice a week; no one to tell you what time to go to bed and what time to get up; no Miss Read to tell your troubles to, no one to come into your dormitory to smell your breath for alcohol every night on your

117

return from a night out with your mates; no more rules and restrictions. This was the last stop before you were released into the world, a sort of last-chance hotel. Well, the time did arrive for me to leave, but not before I tried to enter the armed forces. Yes, once again I had lost my job, this time at the store in town, and in desperation I decided I was going to join the army. I suppose it was that feeling of uncertainty and insecurity, of not having a job that would last, and the prospect of surviving out there on my own, so I applied to join the army. I went to their careers office, got all the information and sat the exams. I got as far as the medical but unfortunately I failed that because I had flat feet. Well, I thought, I was a good swimmer so I applied to join the navy. But I didn't have it all up there in the head to pass the exams, so my last attempt found me applying to join the merchant navy. This time I passed all the exams as well as the medical, and the final sign-up papers arrived at the hostel.

I was called into the superintendent's office. Mr Culshaw was sitting at the desk when I walked in.

'Come in and sit down, Ned.' I was still referred to as Ned; over the years it had stayed with me. 'Your sign-up papers for the merchant navy have arrived. Here they are. All you have to do is sign on the dotted line. Here's a pen. But before you take it and sign, let me ask you something. Why are you doing this?'

I told him I wanted to travel and see the world.

He looked at me and said, 'That's not a good excuse for joining the merchant navy. You see, Ned, you have to remember — and never forget — what your life has been like right up to this very moment, when you first came into care at the age of seven. Your life has been ruled by nuns telling you what to do. You attended school and were told by your teachers what to do. You went to numerous foster homes and again you were told what to do. You were in a succession of children's homes and you were still told what to do.

'Now, do you think that if you sign this piece of paper it will change your life for the better? There are only so many portholes and doors you can go through on a ship, whereas on land there are thousands of doors, and any one of those can change your life. If you go away to sea, that's all you will see for weeks, sometimes months, on end, and you will always be taking orders, sometimes from people who are younger than you. So what do you want? Have no chance at sea or have as many chances as you can take on land?'

I thought about what he was saying, all at sea, in and out of the same doors weeks, sometimes months, on end, even taking orders. And no girls. I raised my head and met his gaze.

'Keep the pen, Mr C. I'm going to take my chances on dry land.' And with that I got up, shook his hand, then turned and walked out of the office. I went back to the sitting room, sat down with the other lads and resumed watching *Top of the Pops*. I thought some more about

119

what Mr C had said and came to the conclusion that this man was only looking out for me. I realised that, for the first time in my life, someone was thinking about me and about my future welfare, not wanting to give me orders but chances.

16

The first place I was taken to was Mrs Knights' board and lodging house right in the middle of Scotland Road, a predominantly white area right next to Anfield, Liverpool FC's ground. It was an area I had heard about all through my time in care, stories of fights between the Shines and the Scotty Road gangs, so I was somewhat perplexed as to why they would want to deposit me in an area such as this. It was like going into red-neck country. The digs were on the fourth floor of a tower block. After dinner — liver, mash and peas, or something like that — I'd retreat to my room and play music, mainly soul and Tamla. Sometimes after dinner I'd go downstairs to the big courtyard and play football with some of the other lads who lived in the block and around the area. On Saturdays I'd be in my room and hear this almighty roar coming from Anfield. To be honest, it put the fear of God into me; it was so loud I thought a lynch mob was at the door. Needless to say, my stay there didn't last — maybe I'd played the music too loud — and the authorities were called once again. I was finally moved to lodgings right back in the heart of Liverpool 8, where it had all started.

This move back to Liverpool 8 went a little way towards easing my anxieties, although I did feel a little out of sorts on my arrival there. A slight uneasiness and uncertainty came over me;

I had not grown up here, and coming back to live here might turn out to be even harder than living outside it had been for the last ten or so years. When we'd been taken away from 'the Eight' ten years earlier there had been a strong sense of community. But ten years on, the deprivation and squalor were plainly visible, and now here I was going through one of the many doors on offer: this one was my bedsit, a single room consisting of a double bed, wardrobe, small kitchen table and a sideboard. The kitchen was the size of a shoe box and the toilet was on the landing below. My landlord was Mr Spencer, a small man who always wore a pork-pie hat and a mac, a very easy-going and pleasant sort of chap. He was quite relaxed about the rent too; if I fell behind I could pay him an extra pound on top of the usual rent and so not leave me too broke.

Settling back into 'the Eight' turned out not to be too stressful in the end. I was already familiar with the area and I was living just around the corner from Hatherley Street, where I'd stayed with Auntie Dolly. I seldom walked down that street because of memories of Mary beating me when I ran away, but it didn't stop me from frequenting the old haunts where I used to play, and all the other streets and houses that I may have passed through when I was a toddler.

Getting back in touch with my brothers and sister was foremost in my mind. I now knew that Claudette was living in a flat somewhere in the area, Michael was still living in Huyton with Mrs

Meakin, Ben had gone off to HMS *Indefatigable*, his naval training establishment, and Brian had joined the army. The family was still scattered but at least I had an idea of where they all were. Mr Andrews, the welfare officer from the early days, had given me Claudy's last known address and I had tracked her down. I was really happy to see her. She still looked the same and I thought that this was going to be the start of us all getting back together again. She had also made me an uncle as she had just given birth to a baby girl.

There was another surprise addition to the family. I found out that we had a younger sister living just around the corner from Claudette, and it happened quite by accident. I was out walking with my mate Ray and we passed a road with small tenement-like flats, with little balconies at the front.

'See that young girl standing next to that woman?' said Ray, pointing to a young girl standing next to an older white lady on one of the balconies.

'Yeh.'

'That's your younger sister.'

I looked at him blankly for what must have seemed like ages, then stammered, 'What?'

'Yes, your mum had another baby, after you were born and when you were very small. She gave your little sister to that lady standing next to her. Give her a wave. Go on, give her a wave.'

I gave her a tentative wave and shouted, 'Hi'. The lady standing next to her shouted back, 'Clear off'. We went round to our Claudette's to

123

ask her if she ever knew that we had another younger sister. She said, 'All my life I have heard rumours that we had another sister, but could never substantiate them.' A few days later I went round to see this young sister again, along with Ray, only this time making sure her mum wasn't around. We shouted for her to come to the corner of the street, and it was then that we were formally introduced. Her name was Lorraine and she was just about to leave school. We chatted for a while and asked each other lots of questions. She was a year younger than me so I was no longer the baby of the family, but the fact that was hard to accept was that she hadn't had to grow up in care. Why not? Why hadn't Mum ever brought her to see us when we were at the convent? Who was this other woman she called Mum? Why couldn't we have stayed with her too? It felt like me, Claudy, Brian and Michael had just completed a long sentence and our youngest sister had got away with it scot-free. I know it wasn't her fault, but I couldn't help feeling we'd collectively drawn the short straw.

The next time I saw Ben he was in a much better state than when I'd seen him with his face all messed up. He had now left the *Indefatigable* and the navy, and joined the army, but I was not aware at the time that he was AWOL. He would take me nightclubbing at weekends and we'd get stoned, and he even managed to get a membership card for the Cavern, the club where it had all started for the Beatles and so many others. Ben had a friend called Alvin and we all started to hang out together.

One day Ben asked me if I'd go with him to pick up a parcel from Edge Hill station later that evening. I agreed and he told me not to forget to wear something dark. I didn't think too much about this odd request. As we were climbing over the wall I asked him just exactly what it was we were going to pick up.

'I don't know yet,' he said, 'and keep your voice down.'

We made our way to a platform packed with parcels and he told me to start going through them.

'But what am I looking for?'

'Anything that looks interesting,' he replied.

I heard a whispered shout for me to get my head down. Ben pointed to a railway night watchman who was coming towards us along the platform. He passed by and we carried on rummaging. Then suddenly Ben shouted, 'Paddy, get the fuck out of here.' I looked up and saw all these policemen with dogs. I dropped everything and ran as fast as I could. Ben was close behind and I could hear him saying, 'Keep going, our kid. I'm right behind you.' We got back to the flat, fell about laughing, then got changed and made our way to the Cavern.

17

A friend of Alvin's had told us about an employment agency called Manpower, which was based in Manchester. He said a group of lads from 'the Eight' were going to sign up as there was the immediate guarantee of work. Alvin wasn't able to come straightaway but Ben and I decided to give it a go. We were based in Immingham, near Grimsby, although the job was in Hull, and involved red-leading pipes connected to massive oil containers.

The nightlife in Immingham was non-existent and going home to Liverpool for the weekend was out of the question, so we had to create our own entertainment. Sometimes in the evenings some of the lads would get up on stage in the mess hall and sing a couple of songs for the rest of the workers. One Saturday morning one of the lads went into town to buy some of the latest sounds from the local record shop; he returned a few hours later clutching an album. It had a brightly coloured cover, mostly red, green and yellow, and across the top was the word 'Hair'.

'You've got to listen to this,' he enthused as he put it on my record player that Alvin, who turned up a week later, had brought up for me. Well, most of the music the rest of the lads had brought with them consisted mainly of Motown, Stax and Atlantic, songs of love and happiness, so when he put this record on my player we sat and listened. At first it took us a while to realise that it was a musical we were listening to and that the songs were all about peace and love, beads and freedom. Then it came to one particular track, a guy singing about being a coloured spade, nigger, and so on. I stood up and told the lad who'd brought the record that I was not prepared to listen to that type of music, especially on my record player, and stuck on some good old Motown. Ben had a more philosophical approach to it; he told me not to get too upset about it, that protest songs came in many forms and that this particular album was actually quite funky.

Little did I know that my first acting role would be in Hair, the very show whose soundtrack I'd refused to listen to. It was only much later that I was able to understand why the words that had offended me were being used and what their purpose was.

When we returned to Liverpool we had so much money in our pockets that we decided to treat ourselves to some new clothes. It was a great feeling handing over cash to the sales assistants for our purchases instead of just stealing them, which we did more often than not. And we couldn't wait to go to the Cavern dressed in our new strides and shirts and blazers. An earlier time at the Cavern I'd met a girl I liked but nothing came of it and she sent me a 'Dear John' letter. She was there that night. I was still feeling a bit cut up about it, but took Ben's advice to accept that people change and their feelings change and that I should just get on with it. In fact, I got on with it so well and drank so much Bacardi that I passed out right in the middle of the dance floor.

After a short while I was back on it again. We now had a regular group of girls we would dance with. We were good dancers so we were popular and they would always be in our corner. Most of the bouncers in the clubs around Liverpool were white and it was no big secret that they resented the idea that young lads from 'the Eight' could come into their clubs have a good time and then leave with 'their' women. The unwritten rule seemed to be that you could come into the clubs and spend your money, but you didn't leave with one of their girls. When things got a bit too heated we stayed away from the city for a while and frequented the local clubs in our own neighbourhood, like the Embassy or the Sink, which, I might add, played the best sounds around, all the latest soul and early ska and blue beat sounds.

18

One day Alvin (always full of ideas) suggested that we should form a group. Ben and I jumped at the idea. We called ourselves Soul Motion. We started to get a few songs together that Alvin had learnt to play on his guitar, songs like 'Up On the Roof', 'It's Alright', 'Then You Can Tell Me Goodbye', 'A Thousand Stars in the Sky', 'This Boy', 'Daddy's Home', 'Blue Moon' and 'Sweet Was the Wine'. We rehearsed every day and, depending on the weather, usually at Alvin's house, in his mother's front room or in the park. It was quite common to see groups rehearsing outside in 'the Eight', clustered on street corners. Some poaching of band members even went on.

While we were practising at Alvin's house one day, he produced some little yellow pills; he said they would help us achieve perfect harmony. Alvin's mum brought us some coffee and as soon as she left the room we popped the pills and carried on playing. We came to the end of a song but Ben wanted to go through it one more time and started to sing the opening lines again. Just before my cue, I told them I just had to sit down for a moment. Then Ben said he had to sit down too and Alvin followed suit. That is the last thing any of us remembered until we were woken up, hours later, by Alvin's mum, who suggested that Ben and I go home. I flopped on my bed and was out like a light. When I woke up I went round to Alvin's. His mum answered the door and I asked her if Alvin was going to come with me to the dole office. She looked at me and in a quiet voice said, 'Paddy, it's still the same day. You were here only two hours ago and you passed out on the settee. You don't sign on till tomorrow.'

I was very nervous when we did our first gig at the A + B Club, even more so because another band which was also performing had recently had a hit with a song called 'These Eyes'. They went by the name of the Guess Who. The moment arrived for us to step on to the stage. We each took a deep breath, paused for a moment and then we broke out into 'Sweet Was the Wine' in perfect harmony, followed by 'People Get Ready' and a medley of other songs. The set went well and we were immediately booked to do a session at a club in Chester. We left the club on a high and celebrated with a meal in the restaurant of the Somali Club on Upper Parliament Street. And now that we were so obviously on the road to stardom we decided to cut down on the cigarettes.

The following day we got ourselves a proper rehearsal space in a local club called Stanley House, another club in 'the Eight', and then accompanied Alvin into town. He wanted to get a new suit. While we were waiting for him to be measured up, Ben said to me in a low voice, 'We should come back here tonight and do this place.'

'What,' I said, 'break in? What are we going to take?'

'These,' he said, nodding towards some jewellery displayed in a cabinet. I looked at the rings, watches and Win cigarette lighters.

'OK,' I said. I was nervous but thought, what the hell. We went back to 'the Eight' and rehearsed some more, but I couldn't stop thinking about what we were going to do. I had never done anything like this before. I hadn't really stolen anything from a shop before, only food and sweets and things like that. I asked Ben if we should wear dark polo-neck pullovers, dark trousers and black pumps again.

'Well,' he said, 'it might help, considering we're both black and it will be dark.'

When we returned later that night we scaled the outside of the building, up the drainpipe and in through the small window overlooking the narrow back alleyway. We had no problem finding the display cabinet and we quickly emptied the swag into a duffel bag. As we were making our way back to the stairs leading to the window we'd come in through I heard a light clicking sound. I stopped and whispered to Ben to do the same.

'I thought I heard something,' I said. We stood motionless for a few seconds and then decided it was nothing. As soon as we started to move off, there was the click again.

'I could have sworn I heard it again.' We both stood still once more. I looked down to where I thought the sound might be coming from and there in the blackness was this bright beam,

131

stretching across the room at almost shin height.

'I think this is what is making that noise,' I said to Ben, waving my hand through the beam and listening to the clicking.

'That's all very good, our kid, but do you think we can get off now?' replied Ben.

'Yeah, yeah,' I said, not able to resist slicing my hand through the beam one more time before easing myself out of the window after him.

As we made our way back we heard voices below us.

'Rozzers!' Ben said. 'Get back up.'

This didn't go down too well with our friends on the ground, who immediately started hurling their truncheons and helmets at us. We roof-hopped our way to the end of the block only to find that the police had called the fire brigade. My heart started to thump as we heard the whirring of the extending ladder making its way up. I held my breath as the torchlights came closer.

'Over here. I think we've found them,' said a voice as the beams settled on us,

'Come on out, lads, your only way off this roof is down this ladder.'

When we reached the ground we were immediately handcuffed and thrown into the back of the Black Maria and taken to Bridewell police station and charged with breaking and entering. But we weren't charged with stealing anything as I had thrown the swag bag back into the building on my way back up on to the roof.

We were subsequently ordered to be detained at Her Majesty's Pleasure for two weeks for reports at Risley Remand Centre on the outskirts of Warrington. Ben and I had ample time to reflect on our behaviour, our past and events leading up to our arrest. We had both learnt a lesson. The harsh reality was that the Risley Remand Centre was yet another institution in what seemed to have been a lifetime of institutions — except this one was a lot harsher than the others. You were locked in your cell for hours on end. You only had half an hour in the prison yard, walking around in a circle, then you were locked up again. We knew we had messed up and that there was an alternative to spending time in and out of prison. We were going to try and do something positive with our lives.

Just before our two weeks were up we appeared before the court again. The report took into consideration that we had both just come out of care and that it was our first offence, and we were released on six months' probation. I walked free from court but Ben was detained as he was AWOL from the army. He had to serve out his sentence in the glasshouse in Colchester. So my own relief was tinged with sadness since I did not know when I would see him again.

19

Shortly after leaving the remand centre I moved into a bedsit just off Granby Street and managed to get a job at Lewis's department store where our Claudette was already working. Lorraine, our new sister, had now moved in with her, Michael was working at the ice rink, close to Edge Hill, and Brian was still in the army, although no one had heard from him for quite a few years.

I was still practising my vocals, even though I hardly ever saw Alvin. Then one afternoon he appeared at the store. He showed me an advert for an audition for a musical; it was being held right now over at the Empire Theatre in Lime Street. Alvin asked me if I would come along to give him some support. I thought, why not, he's a mate, though I did feel a little guilty using my mum as an excuse when I told my boss that she had been taken ill and been rushed to hospital.

We got to the theatre to find only three men there and they looked as if they were about to leave. Alvin asked one of them if the auditions had finished.

'Yes, lads, we're on our way to Manchester now. We'll be doing more auditions there tomorrow at the Palace Theatre.'

Then he turned to his companions and asked if the pianist was still in the building. He was, and Alvin got to audition. I stood by the side of the stage not quite knowing if it was going well for Alvin or not. When he had finished his song there was a lot of murmuring from the three men. Then one of them moved towards the front of the stage and asked me if I would like to sing for them.

Having only gone along to support Alvin, I hadn't been expecting to audition but I said, 'Yes, I'll have a go, but I don't have any music, and I don't know what song to sing for you.'

'Do you know 'Yesterday' by the Beatles?'

Who didn't? I said yes and the pianist started playing the intro to the song. Now, when I was singing with Ben and Alvin I was the one who had to sing the falsetto parts. It had taken its toll and I knew I wouldn't be able to get up that high, and so my voice went all the way down to the basement and stayed there.

I came to the end of the song and the same man asked me my name again and told me he was called David. He then asked me if I could dance.

'Well, I go to the disco, but I'm not great,' I replied, and then showed them my moves, hoping they'd be as impressed as the girls in the Cavern. It seemed to work and David asked me if I would like to come to Manchester the next day as he wanted to see me again. I looked over to where Alvin was standing and smiled at him as if to say, he likes us.

'Yes, we can,' I replied.

I didn't go back to work that afternoon as my mind was all over the place. I kept asking Alvin what did it all mean, and what were we going to do if they gave us jobs, and what about Ben? I went round to Claudette's and told her the news. I didn't have enough money for the train fare to Manchester; so I walked over to the gas meter and emptied the contents when Claudy left the room to get some drinks. She was totally unaware of what I'd done.

When we arrived at Oxford Road station next day, the queue outside the Palace Theatre, which was bigger and grander than the Liverpool Empire, stretched from the stage door for two blocks. We weren't sure if we should go straight in so we decided to join the queue and see what happened. We were slowly edging towards the stage door when I became aware that my name was being called. 'Paddy Barber. Is there a Paddy Barber here?' We went to the front of the line and standing at the stage door was David from the previous day, a big friendly smile on his face,

'Hello, Paddy. Glad you could make it. Come inside.'

The backstage was buzzing with activity. Some kids were practising dance routines, others stood singing round the piano, others were filling out forms. David asked me to sing again, and then do a few simple dance steps with him to a more upbeat number. He was very encouraging and my nervousness gave way to confidence. Suddenly I was dancing and singing at the top of my voice. He urged me let go and to scream at the top of my voice and express a range of emotions. At the end he told me to leave my address and telephone number with the lady at the side of the stage. I told him I didn't have a telephone. The address will do, he said. He thanked me for coming and said he hoped to see me in London . . .

On the way back to Liverpool I continued to bombard Alvin with questions. 'Are we going into show business?' 'Have you been to London before?' 'Are these guys serious about us?' 'What are we going to say to Ben? When he comes out of the glasshouse will he understand if we go off to London? Will he be able to come and join us?' Alvin was a bit quiet, a bit subdued, but I took that to be him just being calm and relaxed about the whole thing. He was always saying to me, 'All right, all right, calm down, calm down.'

David's final words were still ringing in my ears when we reached Liverpool. I said ta-ra to Alvin and walked home. Then I went into the kitchen, put some water in a pan and added a cupful of porridge oats. I added a smidgeon of salt and stirred gently.

The following days just seemed to pass in a blur; they were days of expectancy. I wasn't one for receiving many letters and if I did they were always from the government or the local education authority. Then one day the Post Office kid rang the bell. I thought it was probably for the landlord, but the envelope he carried was for me. I pulled out the telegram and read the contents.

Dear Patrick, please call this number in London as soon as possible, good news. Please reverse the charges, regards J. Verner, Frank McKaye and David Toguri.

★ ★ ★

I couldn't believe it. I ran out of the house and went to Alvin's. Mrs Christie opened the door as I blurted out, 'Is Alvin in, Mrs Christie? I got a telegram and we have to phone London.' Alvin came bounding down the stairs as he too had seen the telegram boy stopping at my place. He put on his coat and we went off to the nearest telephone box. I dialled the number and heard the operator asking if they would accept the reverse charges from a Mr Patrick Barber. Then Mr McKaye came on the phone. He was telling me how impressed they'd been with my audition and then he said, 'We would like you to play the part of Hud in a new rock musical called *Hair*. How do you feel about that?'

My head started to spin with trying to take in what he had said. He had just offered me a part in a show. My heart was pounding. I turned to Alvin and repeated Mr McKaye's words. Alvin looked at me and said, 'What about me? Ask them about me? How did I get on? If they offer you the job don't take it because it will be the end of the group, and the end of our friendship.' I turned back to the telephone and, speaking slowly into the mouthpiece, said it was very good news, that I was excited about it, but how had my friend Alvin got on?

'Well, Paddy,' he said, 'your friend didn't do so well. But we would really like you to come to London and join us.' I looked at Alvin once more, waiting for him to say, go on, Paddy take it; but there was this impassive look on his face,

138

as if he wasn't going to add anything to his last statement. I spoke into the phone once more and said, 'Well, I'm sorry, but we are in a band and we would like to stay together as a band, so I'm afraid I'm going to have say thanks for the offer but no thanks. He's my friend.' Mr McKaye said, 'That's OK. Paddy, I'm sorry about your friend Alvin, but if you should change your mind then call us.' I thanked him and hung up.

We stepped out of the booth and started to walk back to our homes. It was tea time now and as we approached Alvin's house he said, 'I'm going in for my tea now so I will see you later.' I carried on home, made myself a bowl of porridge and then lay on the bed, thinking about what might have been, thinking about our friendship, thinking about Ben. Ben was the one who'd introduced me to Alvin. I hardly knew him. I hadn't grown up with him, but I had grown up with Ben, so I'm thinking all the time — it's friendship that matters, friendship that's important, and that's all that counts. I will go round and see Alvin in about an hour's time.

Mrs Christie let me in and asked how the phone call had gone. I told her that it had gone very well but that I'd turned it down. She wanted to know why. I told her Alvin had said it would split up the group and spoil our friendship.

'Group? What group?' she asked. She reminded me that Ben was away in the army, that I lived alone in a bedsit and Alvin had his family. She also told me that her son wasn't really my friend if he let me turn down an opportunity like this.

139

'You get back on the phone to those people and tell them you want the job.'

I did just that and made the call. As I stepped out of the phone box I thought, this is it. I had just changed my life forever.

I went round to Claudy's to tell her the good news and asked her how was I going to tell Ben. She told me not to worry about him, that he would understand and he'd be one hundred per cent behind me. 'This is a new start for you now, our Paddy, and we are all made up for you and so will Ben be. Just you knock 'em dead when you get there.'

So one morning in January 1970 I started out on my journey to London. I only had one small bag stuffed mainly with my records and I was now sitting on the train waiting for it to leave Lime Street station. A guard on the platform tapped on the window and beckoned me to the door. I pulled down the window and he said, 'Somebody over there wants to say ta-ra to you', pointing towards the barrier. I looked along the platform and saw Alvin. I jumped off the train, ran to him and we hugged. He wished me luck and we just had time to say goodbye before the whistle blew.

★   ★   ★

I couldn't help staring at the man sitting opposite me. His face was so familiar but I just couldn't remember where I had seen him before. I decided to start up a conversation. 'Hi, I'm Paddy Barber,' I blurted as I thrust out my hand.

'I'm going to London to start rehearsals for a new musical called *Hair*.'

He leant across the table and stretched out his hand and quietly said, 'Hi, Paddy, my name is Mike. Pleased to meet you.'

'I don't mean to be rude or anything; I'm sure I have seen you before but I can't quite make out where.'

'I'm with a band called Scaffold,' he said.

I was only sitting across from Mike McGear, a member of one of the big groups in Liverpool at the time (and Paul McCartney's brother, to boot) a group which had had huge hits with 'Lily the Pink' and 'Thank U Very Much'.

When we reached London I took a taxi to Maiden Lane. Mr Verner gave me some money and told me I'd be staying at the YMCA in Great Russell Street. That night I couldn't sleep so I decided to go for a short walk around town. I had never seen so many lights in one place; the shops were still open, there were people coming in and out of restaurants and theatres, nightclubs and discos and there were lots and lots of strip clubs all in a space of a square mile. And the thing that struck me most was that it was so cosmopolitan. I thought I'd hear only London voices but every other voice seemed to be foreign and I hadn't even reached Soho yet, I was still on Tottenham Court Road.

I thought to myself, this is it, this is London. This is where my new life starts.

20

The next morning I made my way to the YWCA, which happened to be in the next street from the YMCA, and made my way to the big hall. The room was alive with a mix of kids from all over England, quite a lot of northerners, too, although I didn't recognise any of them from the auditions. Jimmy Verner and Frank McKaye welcomed us all on board and wished us good luck. Then it was over to David Toguri for introductions. We all sat around in a big circle and David introduced us to each other, one by one. Then we had to go and see the company manager, Bob Gabriel, and give him our names and addresses. We had to register with Equity, the actors' union, and apply for our provisional red licence. You couldn't act on stage without an Equity card: you had to do forty weeks of professional shows, at the end of which you were automatically issued with a full Equity blue card. The tour of *Hair* was to last just over forty weeks. The first day continued with what were called trust exercises, the ones where you shut your eyes and fall backwards into people's outstretched arms, trusting that they will catch you; with touching and feeling people's faces with your eyes closed; and with other theatrical games, all of which was intended to help us gel together and work as one big, happy tribe.

During rehearsals Bob came over to me and

told me that there was already another Patrick Barber somewhere in Equity, and that I had to change my name, so I used my confirmation name, Paul. I became Paul Barber again.

We were going to tour all the major cities in England, starting off in Manchester, and a one-week stint in Aberdeen in Scotland, and ending the tour back in Manchester. There was also a third company, which was to have a permanent base in Glasgow. The rehearsal period was about four or five weeks and during those five weeks I had found another place to stay in Hamilton Terrace, Maida Vale.

Every night after rehearsals we were allowed to go and watch the original cast of *Hair* at the Shaftesbury Theatre, to give us inspiration and a chance to meet them. Peter Straker was playing the part of Hud and Paul Nicholas was in the lead role. Hud was the leader of the black tribe and the first song that I had to learn was 'Coloured Spade', the song I'd taken off my record player back in Immingham. I now understood what the song was trying to say; almost like Cyrano de Bergerac, if you want to call me names I can get in there first and think of far more derogatory names. The whole message of *Hair* was make love not war, and its theme the stance against the Vietnam War in which America was embroiled.

Paul Nicholas joined us for the last few days of rehearsal as he was going to play the lead part in our show for a few weeks to start us off, before returning to the West End. After our final rehearsal we did the performance in front of the original West End cast and afterwards we all got little gifts from our counterparts to wish us luck for the tour.

We had been told that there was a nude scene in *Hair* and that we had a choice as to whether or not to do it. They told us that the stage would be completely blacked out apart from the strobe lighting and that the audience wouldn't really be able to distinguish between male and female. I wasn't really bothered about taking my clothes off. Just as well: it seems as if I've been taking my kit off ever since.

The first night, at the Palace Theatre, Manchester, went down a storm. I was feeling a bit jittery as I waited for the half-hour call in the dressing room: after all, I was about to perform in front of the largest audience I had ever seen. But although my nerves soon disappeared after the audience applauded the first song I still wasn't sure if they would still be there when we returned on stage for the second half.

During the interval, David came round to all the dressing rooms congratulating us all on the success of the first half and told us that the audience was loving every minute of it. People were seeing nudity on the stage for the first time (this pre-dated *Oh! Calcutta!*), and there was a gasp when the cast emerged naked from under the big billowing sheet as we sang 'Where Do I Go', with its refrain of beads, flowers, freedom, happiness. As the last note of the song faded, the audience went wild.

At the end of the show we went down into the audience and led some of them on stage to

144

dance with us. Later on, I worked with one of the guys I'd plucked from the audience. His name was Alan Igbon and we ended up doing a TV show together in 1984 called *The Front Line*.

One night after the show some of us were sitting around listening to music. It was the early hours of the morning and it had become very hot and stuffy in the room. I decided to strip off all my clothes except for my patent leather boots and bowler hat, which were part of my hippy dress at the time. I then said I was so hot I fancied going for a walk, to which someone replied, 'You mean like that?' It then became a dare and they bet me a tenner to walk across the road and back. We trundled downstairs and I opened the door and went to the zebra crossing just outside the house. I walked across, turned round, grinned back at my fellow cast members and started back. No sooner had I stepped off the pavement than a police car pulled up. One of the coppers wound down his window and said, 'Get in'.

I was detained overnight and then put up before the magistrates in the morning. One of them burst out laughing when the policeman read out his statement. I was asked why I had done it and I said that it was for a bet.

'How much was the bet?' was the next question.

'Ten pounds,' I replied.

'Well, you just lost five pounds because that's what we're fining you.'

By the time I got to the theatre that evening it

was in all the papers. I got a short letter of congratulations from the producers of *Hair* saying that I had given the show a real boost with the free publicity.

When we played Newcastle one young woman who got pulled up to dance with us was so overwhelmed about being invited on stage, and so enthusiastic about the show, that she was asked to audition the next day. She ended up joining the cast and continuing on the tour with us. Her name was Angela Bruce. She was so vibrant and full of confidence and we immediately struck up a friendship, which became solid as the tour went on and continues to this day. Angela was always on hand for a laugh and to give me good advice when I needed it. After the touring show finished in Manchester, Angela and I were asked if we would like to join the Glasgow cast, which had been transferred to Blackpool and for some reason — I can't explain why, even now — I developed a bit of an attitude problem towards the other members of the cast and wouldn't socialise with them or make any real effort to be nice to them. Angie took me aside and told me I had to change my behaviour, that whatever my problems were it wasn't their fault. She knew this wasn't the real me and she wanted me to show them that side. Angie's words really moved me and I was deeply touched that she was concerned about me. I'd had too few people like that in my life.

Towards the end of the tour an actor called Dickie Harris had joined the company and during one of the shows, towards the end of the first act, we were under the sheet getting ready for the nude scene. We were undressing when he said something I didn't take too kindly to, so I bopped him one, giving him a black eye just moments before we were meant to emerge from under the sheet, holding daffodils and singing the beads, flowers, freedom, happiness song. We started to sing, looked at each other and burst out laughing. The whole thing was about love and peace and the two of us had just been having a punch-up under the sheet, not exactly practising what the song was preaching. From that day on we were inseparable.

At the end of the last night in Blackpool the show finally came to an end and I suddenly found myself at a loss as to what to do next. I was in all honestly a bit unsure about calling myself an actor. I wasn't sure whether or not to return to Liverpool and sign on the dole, but somehow I felt that if I did go back I would consider myself a failure. So, like any other actor who didn't have another job to go to, I bought the *Stage* paper and turned to the back pages. I came across a job advertising for a stage manager at the Talk of the Midlands in Derby. I applied for and got it, even though I didn't know much about stage management. The Talk of the Midlands was a variety club and many stars passed through the doors during my time there, among them Frank Ifield, the Merseybeats, the Black Abbots, Peter Gordino, Norman Wisdom, Max Wall, Frankie Vaughan, Gene Pitney, Johnny Hachett, Des O'Connor, Les Dawson and Roy Castle. I had a fun time working there with all these stars, and my job was to look after them and see that their dressing rooms were kept clean and tidy. I made sure they got their drinks for the interval, be it a cup of tea or glasses of port for their voices, and to set the props for their acts on the stage.

The late Les Dawson, whom I had met earlier that year in Blackpool, was very pleased to see me again and early one evening before his show he called me up to his dressing room. He wanted to know what I thought about a new piece he was working on. He went into this long monologue about the mother-in-law and by the time he had come to the end of it I was rolling about on the floor. Another star, now sadly gone too, was Roy Castle. On his first night at the Talk of the Midlands he asked me to set his bagpipes on the table down on the stage. He told me to be very careful; they had been in his family for years and were irreplaceable. As I reached the foot of the stairs, I don't know quite what happened but the bagpipes came apart in my hands. All the little pipes just fell out of the bag and went crashing to the floor. I was mortified. As I bent to retrieve the parts now scattered all over the floor, I was panicking as I tried desperately to get everything back into the bag. Then I looked up to the top of the stairs to see if anyone had seen me, only to see Mr Castle doubled over with laughter. 'It works every time,' he said.

21

While I was still working in Derby I received a call from Bob Clench, the company manager of the West End production of *Hair*, asking me if I would like to join the cast in London. 'Would I?' So once again I packed my bags and was back off to the smoke. Finding a place to live wasn't a breeze, though. I made an appointment to visit somewhere that had advertised a vacancy, only to be told by the woman who answered the door that the room had gone. The reply was so quick that I thought, something's up here. I let an hour pass then called the number again and asked if she had a vacancy. She did. Well, nothing wrong with my accent; it must have been something else.

Word was going around among the cast that a new musical was opening in 1972 called *Jesus Christ Superstar*. I turned up for the audition and sang a song but unfortunately I didn't do so well and I knew it. So I hung around at the stage door and, waited for the MD to leave and as he approached me, heading out of the door, I grabbed his arm (not a nice thing to do to a stranger) and I asked him if it was possible for me to have a second try. He was very polite and said, 'Of course. Why don't you come back in two days' time and in those two days you could learn this Caiaphas piece.' So I returned to my squat that evening and set about learning the piece. I had bought the original studio recording of the musical so was able to sing along with the record. Two days later I was back on stage. This time I was a lot happier with myself; I felt I had really made an effort. About a week later I heard that I had got a part as chorus and to be first understudy to Caiaphas, the high priest. Weeks later, when the casting was finally complete, rehearsals got under way, at the London Welsh Centre just off Chancery Lane. Once again I found myself working with Paul Nicholas, who was playing Jesus.

I eventually moved out of my squat and got a place in West Hampstead, along with another actor friend, Larrington Walker, who was also in the show. Anthony Bowles had found it for us and it was owned by the Church. He told me that if my first audition had been as good as my second I could well have been first choice for Caiaphas. As it was, I was quite happy to be understudy, and I did have plenty of opportunities to play the part when the original actor, George Harris, was on holiday and when he got a part in a movie. He eventually left and I took over for the remainder of the show. Meanwhile, my friend Angela was still in the West End production of *Hair*. She had also managed to get a part in a television play which was being directed by Gordon Flemyng for Granada TV, and he was looking for a leading man. Angela asked him what he had in mind.

'I'm looking for a tall, mixed-race kid with a Scouse accent,' he said.

'Oh, that would be Paul Barber. He is in *Jesus*

Christ Superstar,' replied Angela. She then called to tell me that I had an audition and came with me on the day. After I'd read for Gordon he asked me to wait a moment while he disappeared into another office. He emerged a few moments later and said to me, 'Congratulations. You have got the part.' My knees began to buckle. I couldn't speak as Angie gripped me by the arm and steadied me all the way to a coffee bar in Tottenham Court Road while I tried to take it all in. My first television part and it was the lead as well, in an Alun Owen ITV Playhouse called *Lucky*. And it was all going to be shot in Liverpool, my home town.

My own good fortune now gave an opportunity for my understudy to play Caiaphas. I went to see my company manager, Peter Gardner, to tell him the news and ask permission to take the four weeks off I'd need to do the play. He wished me all the best and gave his consent, adding that the part would still be mine when I returned. I truly did feel lucky.

A week later I was back in Liverpool filming. The story was about Sam 'Lucky' Ubootu, a young petty thief who has just got out of prison and is making his way back home to his mother's. She lives alone now because her man (Lucky's father), a merchant seaman, has left home and gone back to sea. On his first day out of prison, Lucky bumps into an old friend who, in his absence, has done rather well for himself and is now driving a flash American car, a Mustang, like the one Steve McQueen drove in *Bullitt*.

He spends most of the day with his friend before finally getting home to his mum, who isn't too pleased to see him. Towards the end of the day he decides to get out of Liverpool and go in search of his father. He goes to the Pier Head and stows away on one of the boats which he thinks will take him to Africa and his father. But he gets found out and is arrested by the port authorities and the police, only to discover that the boat wasn't bound for Africa anyway. It was the local ferry to Belfast.

One of the first things I was to learn about filming for television was never to be late. All the time I was there I was staying in digs in Manchester. I would be picked up from the digs and driven to the studios, and from there the cast would be taken in the Granada bus to the location in Liverpool. One morning I overslept. By the time I arrived I was late. Gordon was on the set, ready to shoot, and he turned to me and said in his low Scots accent, 'You have just cost this morning's shoot Four. Thousand. Pounds.' I was gobsmacked. He only had to say it the once, and every day from then on I was first on the set.

One day Gordon asked me, 'Do you know what rushes are?'

'No,' I said. 'Some kind of bush?'

He laughed and said, 'Come with me when we've finished filming for the day and I'll show you.' This was the third day of filming, so that early evening we went back to the studio. He took me to a small viewing theatre and there we watched the shots from the first and second days.

'Do you see that shot there?' Gordon asked. I nodded. 'Well,' he said, 'do you think you can do it better?'

I looked at it once more and said, 'Yes, of course I could do it better.' He said, 'Fine, we will do that shot again tomorrow. Now you need never go to rushes ever again, so when you're in front of a camera always make sure it's your best.' Once the filming had been completed and everything was in the can Gordon said for the last time, 'It's a wrap.'

I came back down to London and took up my part in *Jesus Christ Superstar* again. On the night *Lucky* aired, one of the cast I was sharing a dressing room with brought in a portable television and in between scenes in the show we would all race back to the dressing room to watch it. The reviews the following morning were more than positive.

I continued to play Caiaphas for a few more years until I had the urge to move on, despite the comfort of having a regular wage. So I decided to leave, knowing I had no job to go to immediately. I had signed with an agency and had been taken on days after the ITV Playhouse went on air in 1974 and my agent wasn't too keen on me leaving the show. But I stood my ground and made it clear that I wanted to take my chances and see what would happen next. Once again I was banking on something turning up.

I was given a big send-off and received a nice telegram from Tim Rice, Andrew Lloyd Webber and David Land thanking me for three years' hard work and talent.

In the two years since leaving Liverpool I had often thought about my mum, and the rest of my family. Ben and Pauline had got married, Brian had enlisted in the army, Claudette had moved to Manchester and Michael had remained in Liverpool. Alvin, my friend from the band, was going out with Lorraine.

I'd had a bit of a scare while I was still in *Superstar* when I got a call telling me that Brian was dead. I just couldn't believe it and didn't know where this information had come from. I quickly rang his base and was told he was alive and well and in the kitchen at the officers' mess. I was so relieved to hear Brian's voice, and we arranged to meet immediately. It was the first reunion in quite a long time.

The second emotional reunion was with Paul. I was doing a series for Granada TV in the mid-eighties called *The Brothers McGregor*, and living in Willesden, north-west London, at the time. One day I received a letter from Granada TV; inside it was another letter from a very young girl asking them if the actor playing in the series was her uncle. She went on to describe how her father had one night informed her that the man on the TV might be related. I didn't need to read any further. I just looked at the address, dropped everything I was doing and immediately made arrangements to go to Runcorn.

My heart was racing as I approached Runcorn; it was racing even faster as I got to his house. I got out of the car, walked up to the front door, knocked and waited. No response. I knocked again.

Just then a neighbour from across the way came over and asked who I was looking for. I told her I was the brother of the man who lived in there and that I had come to surprise him as we hadn't seen each other for a very long time. She told me that he had probably gone to pick his children up from school and gave me directions.

As I stepped just inside the entrance to the school, there he was, Paul, dressed in an overcoat, dark trousers and wellington boots. I saw him before he caught sight of me because he was looking the other way. I didn't say a word. I was only inches away from him and I wanted to see the startled look on his face when he did finally look my way. He didn't disappoint. The moment he turned towards me and focused on my face, it was as if everything else on his mind that day completely evaporated. He stared at me momentarily, open-mouthed, and in those few seconds I could see his eyes grow big and begin to well up with tears. He came towards me, his arms open wide, and we stood there for what seemed like an age, just hugging each other.

Paul gave me his keys and told me to go back to the house and wait there. He wanted to give Reanne and Simon, his children — my niece and nephew — the surprise of their lives. I wanted it to be a surprise, too, particularly for Reanne, whose letter to me had been delivered to Granada TV. I wanted to see the pleasure she

155

would get in having her letter answered in such a way.

I had my back to the door when the kids walked in. Reanne was the first to see me. Without a word she burst into tears, ran over to me and jumped into my arms. Simon was hot on her tail; he too ran to me, arms outstretched, then both of them were smothering me with kisses and cuddles. Paul stood back, watching, a big, beaming smile on his face.

This was one of the happiest moments of my life. I couldn't wait to tell the rest of the family. I now knew where everyone was living so my next plan was to organise a reunion, get everyone together — including the children of my sisters and brothers — under the same roof for the first time in years. I stayed the night with Paul. We all spent hours talking about the rest of the family and it was a really nice feeling. Somehow I felt I was back home. I had found the link in my life that had been missing for so long.

I was determined that, from this point on, I was not going to let Paul and his kids out of my life again.

22

I auditioned successfully for a *Play for Today* called *Gangsters*. Written by Philip Martin and directed by Philip Saville, it was to be shot in Birmingham. My character was called Malleson, a real baddie, playing opposite Maurice Colbourne, Liz Cassidy, Saeed Jaffrey and Ahmed Khalil. It aired on TV to rave reviews and weeks later BBC Pebble Mill was given the go-ahead to make a complete series. It actually went into a third series, reaching cult status.

I remember once during the filming of one of the episodes (I forget the director's name) when I got a bit too big for my boots. We were on location at the almost finished Birmingham NEC and the director asked me to do a particular scene the way he wanted, a not unreasonable request. I turned to him and said, 'I don't think my character would do that.' He just looked at me and said, 'Well, fuck off home then!' There was no answer to that. Needless to say I did exactly what he originally asked me to do and got on with the scene. I made a mental note: don't ever get above yourself; one, it's not worth it, and two, you'll only make a prat of yourself.

I returned to London after it was all over and settled down to some more stage work. My first fringe play was in 1979 for Barrie Keeffe at the Soho Poly, founded and run by Verity Bargate. It was my very first serious role, a lunchtime play called *SUS* (Suspects Under Suspicion), a hard-hitting piece about a young black man accused of killing his wife. The play toured all the major cities up and down the country, playing a lot of universities and social clubs. Barrie Keeffe had also written a film, *The Long Good Friday*, which was in production at the time, starring Bob Hoskins. He asked me to go along to the location where they were filming and see John Mackenzie, who gave me the part of Errol. I turned up at the location in Brixton where my scene was to be shot and was immediately told to go and wait in a bar on the corner while they finished off some other shots. They would get to my scene after lunch. When lunch was over it was my turn to get ready for the shot. I didn't need a costume as I would be naked in bed; later in the scene I would be dragged out of the bed and escorted to the kitchen where Bob Hoskins and Razors, played by P. H. Moriarty, would question me. Bob was very generous and patient with me. Before long, it was all over, the scene was shot and in the can. I had completed my first full-length feature film. What followed months later was a cast and crew showing of the film, then its actual premiere in London's Leicester Square.

Over the next few months I was offered various small parts on television, and even pantomime at Watford, where I played the genie in *Aladdin*. I appeared on TV in the new series, *The Return of the Saint*, starring Ian Ogilvy, and in *Mixed Blessings* and *To the Manor Born*.

These parts came intermittently and in the weeks and months, even years, in between I was signing on the dole, occasionally bumping into the odd actor at Lisson Grove unemployment office. There was a joke going round at the time that the cubicle in which the actors signed on was adorned with fairy lights, and everyone knew it as the luvvies' cubical.

There were times when I would get really depressed because of the long gaps between acting jobs. I would get so disappointed when I went for an audition for a part and didn't get it. My depressions got so bad that at one point I went out and bought some make-up and painted my face white. My girlfriend came home, took one look at me and burst into tears. I very quickly realised that this was not the way to go about it and that something would come along. When something did come up the casting directors would more often than not tell me I was good, but not right for a particular part, and confusion would once again creep in. I would say to myself, well, if you are telling me that I'm good, then why am I not working?

I wrote to a very well-known theatre in Liverpool and asked them if it was possible for me to join their rep company. They wrote back to me on a postcard saying, 'Dear Paul, the next time we stage *A Taste of Honey* we will be in touch.'

At one point I had been out of work for so long that I decided to look for a day job. I went for an interview at a small packing firm and was in the boss's office when he said to me, 'You

159

know, Paul, one day you could be sitting in my chair!' I knew then that it was not for me and quit after a day. I also went for a job on a building site. I turned up on site and went to see the foreman. He took one look at me and asked me to show him my hands, which I did. Then he asked me to turn them over so that he could see the palms. He could see I'd never laid a brick in my life and in not too many words told me where to go. It was soul destroying.

Work did eventually turn up: a new comedy series called *The Brothers McGregor* which was set in Liverpool and was about two brothers, Cyril (Philip Whitchurch) and Wesley (me), one white and the other black, who sold second-hand cars. It was quite popular and we did about three or four seasons.

23

It was during that time that I decided to do some research about Mum. I went to the records office where I discovered that my mother was one of twins — she had had a brother — and had been born in Middlesbrough. I took a morning train up to Teesside and arrived in Middlesbrough in the early afternoon. I checked into a B&B which just happened to be right next door to a social club. The landlady invited me to the club in the evening since I had nothing to do; she told me that there would be a cabaret featuring a group of singers from up north. 'They're very good,' she said. 'A bit like the Drifters.'

Later on that evening, when I was waiting for the group to appear, the compere asked me if I would be offended if he announced my presence. I said I wouldn't, and the next thing I knew he was on stage with mic in hand, announcing that someone had left a car in the car park stacked up on a pile of bricks. 'We think it could belong to Paul Barber, a gentleman otherwise known as Wesley McGregor, sitting at the back. A big hand for Paul Barber, ladies and gentlemen. Stand up, Paul, and take a bow.'

He even got me up on stage to sing a song that I had sung in one of the episodes and I spent the rest of the evening signing beer mats. Later on, a guy came up to me, introduced himself as Mike, and asked what I was doing in Middlesbrough. I told him that my mother had been born there and that I wanted to find out if the house she was born in was still standing. He asked me the name of the street Mum had been born in and I told him Tyne Street. He told me that it might not be there any more but he would pick me up in the morning, take me to the area and show me round.

The next morning, Mike drove me to Tyne Street, in the St Hilda's area of the city, where Mum had been brought up. The old houses had long gone but a few of the pubs were still standing. We decided to stop off at one of them for a pint — in fact, we stopped off at quite a few of them. There seemed to be a pub on every corner. It struck me, as we went from pub to pub, that, despite most of the old houses and steets being knocked down — to make way for new houses and new pubs — there was still a sense of community. I tried to imagine what it must have been like living there; I imagined Mum walking up and down the very streets I was walking down now; imagined the local pubs as they had once been. I thought to myself, I wonder if Mum's parents sat in any of these pubs, night after night. I wonder if they sent her out to any of the shops that are still standing. I was almost inviting déjà vu, thinking to myself, have I been here before? But I knew I hadn't. There were stories flying around that Mum had gone back to Middlesbrough not long after she had given birth to Paul, she hadn't been allowed back in the house, and that her parents didn't want to know her. She had stayed with a friend a few streets away.

In one pub Mike told an elderly man that I was looking for information about my mother, Margaret Bartley. It turned out that he knew a Peggy Bartley — then he went out to fetch her. I was stunned. The fact that Mum had a sister was news to me; but it also meant that she was my auntie. Why hadn't I known about this earlier? Why had it taken so long for me to find out about her? How come the rest of the family knew nothing about Mum's sister?

It was a bit hard for me to take in all this info at once. I wasn't sure how I was going to handle this. What were we going to talk about when she arrived? My mind was racing. I knew I had lots of questions to ask, but would she be forthcoming with the answers? Were there any more members of the family still around?

While we waited, Mike told me a bit more about the place, what it had been like in the early days. He was just telling me about the Middlesbrough Transporter Bridge just around the corner from Tyne Street, now a famous landmark, when the old boy returned with a small lady in her late fifties or early sixties. She came towards me and, as I stood up, she wrapped her arms around me and burst into tears. It was almost as if she had been waiting ten years for this moment to arrive, as if I really was a long-lost relative. I went back to the bar and ordered some more drinks.

When we settled down to chatting, it transpired that she could only remember small bits about Mum; she too had been a bit of a wild child and was always in conflict with her parents, although, unlike Mum, she had not been put into a home. We chatted and spoke fondly of Mum but I was a little disappointed that she didn't have any pictures of Mum or of their parents. I had my camera with me and took a few photographs of Peggy Bartley. I still had a fading image of Mum in my head. I didn't think they looked alike.

24

Work, meanwhile, had eased off again after *The Brothers McGregor*. Although a few good parts came up, I always seemed to be playing the same role and I found that frustrating. I could do accents but only northern ones. I wasn't good with West Indian, or even Jamaican, accents, and I'm still lousy at them now. That was one of the reasons I wanted to do rep, to gain experience of doing other parts and possibly learn other accents. I did audition for the Royal Shakespeare Company, but, alas poor Scouser, I wasn't successful.

But my Scouse accent did prove lucky when I auditioned for *Only Fools and Horses*. As soon as Ray Butt (director and producer) heard me speak he decided that I was the man to play Denzil. I had great fun doing this series. In one episode we were just about to shoot the scene where I slap Del Boy's (David Jason) hand in the park while he is holding a butterfly. In the original script I was supposed to be walking past Del with a ghetto blaster over my shoulder and then slap hands. Thinking about it in the pub, I told Ray that I thought it would be better on roller skates, so that by the time Del looked up from the squashed butterfly in his hand I would be well out of sight. Ray sent me off to the props rooms. Soon after, the weather got worse and as a consequence I had to practise roller-skating in the snow for two weeks before we got round to reshooting the scene. It worked like a dream and I felt so proud.

Ray told me to keep the skates.

When we did the Christmas special, *To Hull and Back*, the one about the diamonds in Amsterdam, in 1985, Ray asked me, 'Can you drive?'

'Yes,' I replied.

'Can you drive one of *them*?' he asked, pointing to a ten-ton truck.

'No, and I don't have an HGV licence either,' I said. He told me not to worry as the real driver would be in the truck, out of shot. All I needed to do was to get in the truck and drive. Needless to say it had sixteen gears so you can imagine what the engine sounded like going across the Humber Bridge in third. Ray took chances with all of us all the time and the end result was invariably perfect. He made you feel special, and I admired and respected him. I still do to this day.

At the end of the Christmas special Ray and John Sullivan, the writer, asked me if I would like to be a member of the gang, which meant being in the show more regularly 'Yes, please, guv,' I replied, and that was that. Denzil became a part of my life for the next years.

The next big movie I did after *The Long Good Friday* was *The Full Monty* and I had to audition for Peter Catteneo. I wasn't hopeful as I wasn't having much luck with film interviews, so I wasn't very enthusiastic about going to see him. It was a low-budget movie and, because I was so used to being rejected, I wasn't too bothered if I didn't get the part.

So, when Peter asked me to read the part where Horse is in the telephone box discussing the penis enlarger with the person on the other end of the phone, I did it quite quickly, just to get it over with. Just so that I could go back home and say to myself, well, that's another useless interview out of the way. I really was in that frame of mind. I was surprised, then, when my agent called me the following day and said that Peter wanted to see me again, only this time dressed in an old suit and looking a bit older. Apparently I looked too young and clean-shaven. My agent told the casting lady that every time I went into her office I looked like a sack of shit.

So I put on an old suit, as requested, and I managed to get hold of a vibrator and attached it to a sealant gun, put it into a plastic bag and went off to see Peter Catteneo again. He asked me to read the telephone sequence one more time, but I didn't show him what was in the bag until I was halfway through the telephone conversation. When I got to the part where I had to say 'It's not working', I pulled out the sealant gun and pressed the trigger so that the vibrator shot out of the gun. As I said the words, Peter calmly, slowly, buried his head in his hands. Then he looked up at me and smiled.

'Can you grow a beard?'

'Yes,' I said.

'Will it be grey?' he asked.

'Yes, it will be white,' I replied.

'The part's yours. See you in seven weeks.'

When we did the strip scene in *The Full Monty* I was a bit nervous. Even though I'd appeared naked before, in *Hair*, I had been practically indistinguishable from all the others, especially under the spare stage lighting. But this was being performed in front of a real live club audience and it was quite clear who was who. We rehearsed the scene over and over again, stopping just before we were meant to throw our police hats into the air, and the people in the club assumed that this was as far as we were going to go.

But Peter had other ideas.

Just before the very last take he came backstage with a tray of glasses and a large bottle of brandy. He told us that this was the one. The audience would think that we would stop in the usual place but this time we were going all the way. We were to throw the hats into the air, count to ten in our heads and then leave the stage. That would be it. One take.

The rest is history.

In the film there is a scene in which Robbie Carlyle's character Gaz is trying to explain to his son Nathan, played by William (Whim) Snape, that he needs to borrow a couple of bob to try and get some capital together to get this strip show on the road. Nathan's immediate reaction to this is to take his savings book to the Post Office and cash in his savings. Gaz tries to stop him but Nathan says, 'You said you'd get it back.' Gaz replies, 'I know but you don't want to listen to what I say.'

'You said so, I believe you,' says Nathan.

Of all the scenes in the film, this one had the greatest effect on me. It struck a chord.

When I was in the car with that man, doing what he asked, and he kept telling me that I was a good boy, I believed him. It's our little secret, he said, and I believed him. When you are young and innocent you believe anything and everything adults tell you. I believed when I was sent to the shops to buy a tin of striped paint. Another time, I believed when I was sent to buy a rubber hammer for glass nails, and a left-handed screwdriver. I believed.

Epilogue

It's now twelve years since *The Full Monty*, and almost thirty years since I left the care system. As I look back on it all, I wonder where would I be now if I wasn't a jobbing actor. Could I have been happier doing something else? I can't really answer that, but what I can say is that, looking back, life has had its ups and downs, just like the bumps I received at Sydney House. I've been in the wrong place at the wrong time but I've also been in the right place at the right time. Life dealt me a hand and this book is a record of that life — the boy I was then, the man I am today.

I think back to the time when I got on the train at Lime Street station all those years ago and found myself sitting opposite Mike McGear of Scaffold. I never dreamt that one day I too would be sitting on a train and someone would come up to me and say, 'Excuse me, are you famous?'

Who would have thought it? A foster kid being famous.

We do hope that you have enjoyed reading this large print book.

Did you know that all of our titles are available for purchase?

We publish a wide range of high quality large print books including:
Romances, Mysteries, Classics
General Fiction
Non Fiction and Westerns

Special interest titles available in large print are:
The Little Oxford Dictionary
Music Book
Song Book
Hymn Book
Service Book

Also available from us courtesy of Oxford University Press:
Young Readers' Dictionary
(large print edition)
Young Readers' Thesaurus
(large print edition)

For further information or a free brochure, please contact us at:
Ulverscroft Large Print Books Ltd.,
The Green, Bradgate Road, Anstey,
Leicester, LE7 7FU, England.
Tel: (00 44) 0116 236 4325
Fax: (00 44) 0116 234 0205

Other titles published by
The House of Ulverscroft:

COULD IT BE FOREVER?

David Cassidy

In 1970, at 20 years old, David Cassidy made his television series debut in *The Partridge Family*, made his first record — the biggest-selling song of the year — and became an idol to millions of people all over the world. He soon became the highest paid solo performer in the world. His recordings sold over 25 million copies and his fan club membership exceeded that of the Beatles. But who was he? Even he didn't know. Now, in his own words, this is David Cassidy's story: his rapid rise to stardom, its rewards and price, the era in which he lived and reigned, the women in his life, his family — and the process of learning to accept himself and his life's path.

IMPERIAL LIFE IN THE EMERALD CITY

Rajiv Chandrasekaran

From a walled-off American enclave of smart villas and swimming pools — known as the Green Zone — the US-led Coalition Provisional Authority, under imperial viceroy L. Paul Bremer III, attempted to rule Iraq in the first twelve months following the fall of Saddam Hussein's regime. Rajiv Chandrasekaran tells the story of the attempt to build American democracy in a war-torn Middle Eastern country. He details not only the risky disbanding of the Iraqi army and the ludicrous attempt to train the new police force, but also brings to light many typical travesties, including the contractor with no previous experience paid millions to guard a closed airport. Chandrasekaran's hair-raising report shows the gap between the Oz-like Green Zone and the brutal reality of post-war Iraq.

PLAYING WITH FIRE

Nigel Havers

When Nigel Havers went to make the film A Passage to India for David Lean, he survived — despite Rex Harrison's prediction that he would die in India. However he had to contend with recalcitrant extras, marauding monkeys and a grumpy Dame Peggy . . . Nigel Havers' memoir takes us from a schoolboy production of A Midsummer Night's Dream to the red carpet on Oscar Night with Chariots of Fire, via starring roles in the West End, classic television series and a cameo in Little Britain. The Hollywood blockbusters that made him a household name are only the beginning. With characteristic modesty, charm and a captivating eye for the absurd, he treats us to the highlights and lowlights of a life like no other.